Is the EU Doomed?

Global Futures Series

'Zielonka offers a new and refreshing vision of Europe's future – one that chimes perfectly with the EU's motto "United in Diversity."'

Giuliano Amato, Former Prime Minister of Italy

'The EU may be not doomed but it is in deep crisis. In this provocative book Jan Zielonka offers an original and controversial proposal for a radically different model of European integration. Challenging conventional views, he considers the prospects of a "neo-medieval" Europe composed of networks of cities, regions and NGOs where a "polyphony" among actors will replace the current cacophony of the centres.'

Josep Borrell Fontelles, former President of the European Parliament and former President of the European University Institute

'Jan Zielonka has written a punchy, incisive and devastating account of the EU and its malaise after the financial crisis. He combines his plea to move away from "sanctimonious Protestant preaching" with a convincing sketch of how a more chaotic pattern of networks between cities, provinces but also a wide range of social and corporate institutions might produce a more durable, effective and legitimate governance. The treatment is eloquent but also wise.'

Harold James, Claude and Lore Kelly Professor in European Studies, Princeton University

'A fascinating and thought-provoking book that will change our view of the EU as neither a true state nor an ever-changing cacophony of nations.'

Josef Joffe, Editor of _Die Zeit_ in Hamburg and Visiting Professor of Political Science, Stanford University

'Jan Zielonka's brilliant analysis of European disintegration is packed with big ideas that are elegantly expressed. It acts as an original and iconoclastic challenge to both the Euro-sceptic and the Euro-federalist discourses on the crisis. This is a must-read book for anyone who cares about the future of Europe.'

Mark Leonard, Director of the European Council on Foreign Relations

'Whether or not you agree with Jan Zielonka's arguments, you will find this book a stimulating read. I'm sure it will provoke much discussion about the future development of the European Union.'

Lord Patten of Barnes CH, Chancellor of the University of Oxford and former European Commissioner for External Affairs

'A brilliant and profoundly original analysis of the European crisis. A work of optimism, as well!'

William Pfaff, author and syndicated columnist

Jan Zielonka

—————

IS THE EU DOOMED?

polity

First published in 2014 by Polity Press

Polity Press
65 Bridge Street
Cambridge CB2 1UR, UK

Polity Press
350 Main Street
Malden, MA 02148, USA

ISBN-13: 978-0-7456-8396-6
ISBN-13: 978-0-7456-8397-3 (pb)

A catalogue record for this book is available from the British Library.

Typeset in 11 on 15 pt Sabon by
Servis Filmsetting Ltd, Stockport, Cheshire
Printed and bound in Great Britain by Clays Ltd, St Ives plc

For further information on Polity, visit our website:
www.politybooks.com

Contents

Prologue

I am a genuine European, by any measure you care to choose, and it gives me no satisfaction whatsoever to conclude that the European Union (EU) may well be doomed. Silesia, where I grew up, was the focus of harsh policies of Germanization and Polonization, so I am not easily seduced by national pride and glory. A Europe without borders was a dream for young people without passports living behind the iron curtain, and for me, personally, integration helped make this dream a reality. I am still a Polish national, but I hold a Dutch passport, own a house in Italy and work at a British university. My working experience with EU institutions has never been thrilling, but it has not been significantly worse than my experience with Dutch or Italian bureaucracies. The EU was a symbol of an integrated Europe, and from the outset I was inclined to give it the benefit of the doubt. Sadly, as my essay explains, at present the EU does not facilitate integration, but impedes it. I therefore propose a radically different concept of European integration with less or no EU.

The European Union was widely regarded as the most successful modern integration project, but it has turned into an embarrassment. It promised to secure prosperity through integration, but it became a symbol of austerity and conflict. It obtained ever-more powers at the expense of national parliaments and governments, but when the global financial crisis erupted in 2008 it proved unable to cope with the social and political disruption that ensued. Powerful shocks spread from the skyscrapers of Manhattan, Canary Wharf and *la Défense* to the corridors of Brussels and to ordinary households across Europe. No wonder so many citizens lost trust in the EU, and that the process of disintegration is gathering pace. But is this decline reversible? Can Europe return to the path of integration under the tutelage of the EU, and, if so, would that even be desirable? Alternatively, if the EU really is doomed, what could and should take its place?

In this essay I argue that the EU will emerge significantly weakened from the current crisis. It will probably survive, but only in more modest form, deprived gradually of major legal powers and political prominence. The currency crisis may well be overcome, but the crisis of socio-economic cohesion and political trust will persist for some time, paralysing EU institutions, generating further conflicts and preventing any substantial reforms.

Contrary to many observers, I believe that the weakening of the EU will not strengthen nation states, but rather lead to the opposite scenario. The EU has helped its members generate growth through its single market and enlargement projects; and it has offered a comfortable excuse for numerous policy failures. A weakening of the EU and its member states will strengthen other political actors such as cities, regions and non-governmental organizations (NGOs). As a result, state borders will be fuzzier, political loyalties will be increasingly divided and administrative jurisdictions will overlap to a much greater extent. I call this phenomenon 'neo-medievalism'.

I will also argue that, contrary to many predictions, the waning of the EU will not lead to chaos and disintegration. Integration will in fact continue, fed by profound economic interdependence, cultural empathy and political pragmatism. However, this will be a new form of integration with no ambition to create a pan-European government. Integration will evolve along functional rather than territorial lines. It will be carried out by various regulatory agencies made up of national and regional governments, large cities and NGOs representing business and citizens. Such diverse and decentralized integrated networks are likely to be more effective and responsive than the current EU, with its rigid rules, dysfunctional central institutions and disconnection from the concerns of citizens and markets.

The essay tries to capture this probable new mode of integration by employing the musical metaphor of polyphony. In the field of music, polyphony is sound and voice with a complex texture, music with parts written against other parts, with several simultaneous voices and melodies. Polyphony does not assume unity and hierarchy, but draws strength and functionality from numerous sets of loose and contrapuntal relationships. So the aim of polyphonic integration would be for Europe's parts to work in greater harmony without losing Europe's greatest treasure: its diversity and pluralism. This mode of integration, whether in the areas of transport, energy, migration, tourism or sport, would be more capable of getting things done, effectively and efficiently. Its competence would ensure its greater legitimacy; and its dispersed and complex polyphonic qualities would ensure its greater resilience when under pressure from future crises. Integration led by the rigid EU dictating 'one-size-fits-all' policies, by contrast, has led to dissonance, rather than harmony. EUphony has become a synonym for cacophony. Through a strange and ironic turn of events, however, present-day disintegration is preparing the way for a new, much more resilient form of integration, whose merits have so far not been widely recognized.

To understand how integration and disintegration work, and why polyphonic integration is the future, we need to look more broadly at power politics in contemporary Europe, exploring the deficiencies of the European social model, capitalism and democracy. In-depth analysis of the EU's byzantine treaties and complex institutional structures will be of little help here. After all, does anyone really believe that the President of the European Commission can determine the fate of integration? Has the Lisbon Treaty been of any use in forging a more coherent Europe? And is the European Parliament channelling Europe's collective political will?

This set of rhetorical questions not only flags up the ineffectiveness of the EU; it also invites us to think about our expectations of what the EU can and should deliver in the second decade of the twenty-first century. The EU always suffered from a 'capability–expectations gap', to use Christopher Hill's expression.[1] It envisioned a model of integration run by a single institutional centre in charge of too many things, with inadequate legitimacy and resources. This vision was unrealistic and destined to fail. So European institutions now need to be sub-divided into smaller functional clubs and networks, and their integrative ambitions need to be scaled down. Integration should not hereon be seen as a remedy for democracy or market failures. Nor should it represent a remedy for greed, selfishness and conflict. But it can offer Europe practical ways of coping with mounting economic, social and security problems that require the cross-border cooperation of many different actors across the whole continent, and beyond. During the past few years, the EU has performed its integrative functions poorly. It now seems unable to reform itself. Integration driven by autonomous functional networks without a strong European centre will in due time be seen as a much more appropriate way forward. The EU may well be doomed, but Europe and European integration certainly are not.

Acknowledgements

This essay greatly benefited from thoughtful comments by Stefania Bernini, Hugo Dixon, Christopher Hill, John Kean, Martin Krygier, Fabian Neuner, George Pagoulatos and four anonymous reviewers. I also benefited from numerous exchanges with graduate students in European Politics and Society at the University of Oxford. The European Studies Centre of St Antony's College has also hosted exciting debates on the topic of this essay.

My gratitude goes also to the European Council on Foreign Relations, which has given me an opportunity to work with some of the brightest European practitioners and experts. I am particularly indebted to Mark Leonard and Dick Oosting for making me part of their fascinating project on the Reinvention of Europe. Special thanks go also to the Institute for Democracy and Human Rights at the University of

Acknowledgements

Sydney, and its director, John Keane, for offering me their institutional hospitality and intellectual inspiration during the writing of this essay.

I would also like to thank Louise Knight and her colleagues from Polity Press for initiating this project and steering it safely to the intended destination.

1

Crisis

'Crisis' is the word we have come to associate with the EU. Yet the origin, nature and implications of this crisis are hotly contested. One thing, however, is certain: this is no ordinary crisis; it cannot be handled in a routine manner by the European Union. As Federico Rampini put it in the Italian daily *La Repubblica*: 'This crisis has assumed dimensions that no one can control. There are too many fires to extinguish in too many diverse places.'[1]

The EU has experienced crises before. In 1965 General De Gaulle refused to attend the European Council's meetings, causing the so-called 'empty chair crisis', which lasted for seven months. In 1999 all twenty European commissioners resigned following allegations of corruption in high places. In 2005 French and Dutch voters delivered a negative verdict on the European constitutional treaty. But there has never been anything like the crisis that began in 2008 and is still unfolding. This crisis is not just about the EU's internal matters. In fact, it was triggered by events far away from Brussels. But the financial storm in New York has quickly spread to many different fields of European politics and society. The EU has attempted to cope with the rapidly evolving situation, but in a clumsy and contentious manner.

If we examine the variety of events that have shaken Europe and the EU over the past few years, we find that there is not one, chiefly financial, crisis but a series of different crises with different spans and durations. The end of one type of crisis may herald the beginning of another. Moreover, all these crises are highly interdependent, albeit in an asymmetric manner. The financial crisis exposed the weakness of several European economies and also of the faulty institutional set-up of the euro and the EU itself. Troubled economies could not but generate political and social consequences. Money has been lost, political careers have been ruined and ideological truths have been challenged as a result of these crises. However, different states and social groups experienced these crises in different ways. Some of them even benefited from Europe's disarray. The EU was not one of the beneficiaries, however. It proved poorly prepared for navigating through the stormy weather and it lost the confidence of Europe's citizens.

European officials are fond of stressing that in the past the EU has emerged stronger from successive crises, but in light of the evidence available at present this rosy history is not likely to repeat itself.

Crisis, what crisis?

One can hardly speculate about the EU's future without getting to the heart of the crisis currently gripping the institution. To put it another way: the cure for a patient begins with a proper diagnosis. The dominant view is that the crisis was about the euro, Greece and sovereign debt. In my view, the most important crisis was and still is one of cohesion, imagination and trust. The latter is obviously harder to address. The hole in the Greek budget is relatively small in aggregate euro-zone terms and could easily be covered. However, Greece is not the only country in financial trouble, few believe that writing off debts will make the Greeks behave like the Germans, and there are no plausible solutions for solving Greece's complex problems. What we do know is that the solutions applied by the EU have so far proved pretty ineffectual. What looked to be a straightforward financial challenge has become a social, political, cultural and even ideological one, concerning the entire continent and not just one 'black sheep'. Let me explain why.

The euro is on the verge of collapse, and the blame is being attributed to external financial shocks and misguided, if not absent, common fiscal policies. The financial discourse has become so prominent that most Europeans have acquainted themselves with the meaning of such ostensibly odd terms as credit crunch, quantitative easing, financial spread, structural adjustments and euro-bonds. However, only some economies within the euro-zone have performed poorly, while others are booming and have faced no fiscal pressures. Can we make any general statements about the euro crisis in this situation? Moreover, it is far from obvious that any fiscal policy would be able to address the roots of the economic problems facing Greece, Cyprus, Portugal, Spain, Ireland and, one may add, Italy. The culture of clientelism and meritocracy can hardly be tackled by macro-economic structural adjustments and budgetary oversight alone. Moreover, fiscal policies alone would not spur the weaker economies to catch up with the stronger ones in a single currency union. A closer look at Greece illustrates this problem.

Greece was a prototype of poor bookkeeping: an unsustainable current account deficit, huge public and foreign debt, a narrow tax revenue base, a ballooning and inefficient public sector, and an untenable burden of pensions and unemployment benefits.[2] However, the country's problems can only partly be explained by the chronic lack of financial discipline. One should also look at the weakness of the Greek state and its administrative structures, at the politics of patronage practised by the two parties ruling Greece since the fall of autocracy, at the economic and political imbalances within the euro-zone system. Ordinary Greeks have probably lived above their means for some time, but, contrary to their depiction in numerous European tabloids, they are not selfish, lazy, uneducated, tax-evading and 'unwilling to embrace change'.[3] Some Greek politicians have cheated their colleagues in Berlin, Paris and The Hague, but they also cheated the Greek people and subsequently lost their confidence.[4] Prior to the crisis the country consumed too much and invested too little, but not all of the current problems of Greece are of its own making. It was not Greece but Germany and France who were behind the faulty design of the European Economic and Monetary Union which envisaged a common currency without any instruments for helping the weaker members of the euro-zone align with the stronger ones. Nor were the Greek banks and their regulators responsible for the global financial meltdown of 2008, which rendered the sovereign debt burden of Greece unsustainable and a tempting target for speculators. From the early days of the euro-crisis, Greece was hardly in charge of its policies, which means that it is difficult to blame Athens for the disastrous social and political effects of severe austerity and internal devaluation. In fact, when in October 2011 the Greek Prime Minister, George Papandreou, announced his intention to hold a referendum on the acceptance of the terms of a euro-zone bailout deal, he was forced to step down from office under the pressure of Germany and other creditor states. Ancient Greek dramas show that a key character can be a perpetrator and a victim at the same time, and this is the case with modern Greece in this crisis.

The stories of Ireland, Portugal and Spain confirm that Greece's economic misfortunes are partly of its own making and partly the result of policies and processes beyond its control. These four states requested a financial rescue from the EU and the IMF, and they were bundled together by the financial discourse under the denigrating acronym PIGS: Portugal, Ireland, Greece and Spain. (Some analysts use PI*I*GS, to include Italy – Europe's notorious debtor.) However, the PIGS' reasons for financial difficulties were not all exactly the same. In 2007 only Greece had a disturbing level of gross public debt: 94.5 per cent of GDP, compared to 25.4 per cent of GDP in Ireland, 36.2 per cent of GDP in Spain. In comparison, the UK's gross debt in 2007 amounted to 43.8 per cent of GDP.[5] Spain and Ireland's major economic problem was a property bubble; this problem was not present in Portugal and Greece. Banks were also in bad shape in Spain and Ireland. The latter went into recession in 2008 after the government had pumped 7 billion euros into its two biggest banks, Allied Irish Banks and Bank of Ireland. Insolvent local banks were not the key problem in Portugal or Greece. The PIGS were weak links in the poorly designed euro-chain. When the pull of financial markets intensified, the PIGS fell off the chain.

Cohesion, imagination, trust

'Ever-closer union' is the official aim of the EU, and the progress of European integration has always been measured by the EU's success in fostering greater cohesion. In the EU discourse, concepts of fusion, convergence, cohesion and integration are often used as synonyms. Over the last few years, however, it has become evident that 'ever-closer union' is a myth, and the EU is facing a profound crisis of cohesion. For instance, unemployment in Greece reached 27.6 per cent in May 2013, continuing an upward trend since the debt crisis erupted five years earlier. In Germany, meanwhile, unemployment was 5.4 per cent, the lowest since the country's re-unification. Outside the euro-zone, Poland has not been in recession since 2008, while Latvia's economy shrank by 25 per cent in 2008–9 (although Latvia, unlike Greece, has recovered relatively quickly). It has also become more obvious than ever that in the EU there are policy-makers and policy-takers, the former exemplified by creditor states and the latter by debtor states. The gap between those within the euro-zone and those outside of it is also widening; the latter have only limited access to the decision-making process affecting their economic interests.

Nobody really knows how to bridge the gap between Europe's powerful affluent centre and its impoverished peripheries. Subjecting all countries to the same set of rules and laws is clearly insufficient.

Central economic redistribution is controversial for practical and ideological reasons. The creation of the single market was accompanied by the creation of a cohesion policy to help the poorer regions cope with the economic competition from the wealthier ones, but the assigned funds were relatively modest and their use and misuse has been widely criticized. Similar cohesion funds were not envisaged with the creation of the single currency. The market was supposed to take care of discrepancies between the weak and strong economic actors within the euro-zone. We now know that this was an illusion. The current situation resembles a joke from the communist era: the state pretends to pay the employees and the employees pretend to work. In the present-day EU the creditor states pretend to subsidize harsh structural reforms and the debtor states pretend to follow the former's directives, however electorally unpopular and economically counter-productive. None of the actors seem to believe that this will ever work, but they lack a plausible solution to address the problem. After all, member states were unable to bridge gaps between their own rich and poor regions despite having budgets the EU could never dream about.[6] Relatively rich states such as Italy are the most striking examples here.

This leads to the next major crisis the EU is

facing at present: the crisis of imagination. Money alone is not likely to get Europe out of this crisis. Europe needs to invent a new way of investing and distributing money, but addressing this paradigm crunch is proving trickier than addressing the credit crunch. Plausible proposals for reinventing Europe and rescuing it from its current malaise are in short supply at present and they are often technical, uninspiring and timid. EU decision-makers are guided by short-term political considerations and are chiefly concerned with defending their own partisan interests, be they national or institutional. EU experts tend to focus on detailed treaties and formal institutions while ignoring historical memories, cultural myths and ideological prejudices. Their abstract modelling and theorizing are increasingly detached from European realities and as such are of little use to Europe's politicians.

However, the lack of a plausible vision for moving the EU forward is also related to broader intellectual and political quandaries. Democracy and capitalism are undergoing a rapid change, which means that understanding Europe and its institutions is not sufficient for addressing current problems. Moreover, solutions for Europe's current troubles can hardly be confined to Europe itself. What happens in China, India, Brazil or the United States will be of paramount importance to the continent's future, and Europeans have a limited understanding of, and influence over, developments in these countries.

Paradigm change takes time. Moreover, new visions, however brilliant, would have to be 'sold' by politicians to the European electorate. At present, the electorate has little trust in politicians, whether they come from Brussels or from national capitals. The current crisis of trust manifests itself not only in opinion polls, but also on the streets of villages and cities. When in the autumn of 2013 the Italian Prime Minister, Enrico Letta, and the President of the European Commission, José Manuel Barroso, visited the tiny southern island of Lampedusa after yet another boat full of migrants sank there, they met an angry crowd of local citizens exasperated by the failure of the EU and their country to stop such repeated tragedies. Likewise, mass, at times violent, protests in the streets of Athens, Madrid or Nicosia are directed at both the EU and respective national governments. Both fare extremely poorly in public opinion polls. According to the November 2012 Eurobarometer, since 2007 trust in the EU had fallen from positive 20 to negative 29 per cent in Germany, from positive 30 to negative 22 per cent in Italy, and from positive 42 to negative 52 per cent in Spain. Public trust in national institutions and politicians is also remarkably low. The Pew Research Center data for 2013 showed that in a relatively affluent France 91 per cent of those polled said that the country's economy was doing badly, up 10 percentage points from 2012. The French were also downbeat about their leadership: 67 per cent thought President François Hollande was doing a poor job in handling the challenges posed by the economic crisis. (Hollande was elected only a year earlier.) Across Europe the established political parties are fighting for their political survival when faced with 'new kids on the block' such as the Greek Syriza party, the Dutch Freedom Party, the Italian 5* Movement or the True Finns. These 'new kids' are hammering not only the national but also the European political establishment.

The way Europe's leaders have handled the crisis has not made them any more popular. It also reinforces the impression that the EU's major problems are cohesion, imagination and trust, and not just poor financial supervision.

Crisis management

EU efforts to handle the crisis have never enjoyed a good press. As Simon Tisdall expressed it in the

Guardian: 'The political bottom line, now as in the past, is that when a full-blown crisis hits, Europe's response falls short. Put another way, when the going gets tough, the EU goes shopping.'[7] Even the remarkable pledge, in July 2012, of the President of the European Central Bank (ECB), Mario Draghi, 'to do whatever it takes to preserve the euro' was greeted by the press in some creditor countries as writing a 'blank cheque' to debtor countries and exceeding the ECB's mandate. Draghi's declaration reassured international markets, though, and averted what seemed at the time an imminent collapse of the euro. Numerous other actions of EU leaders, by contrast, have either failed to reassure the markets or made them pretty nervous. The same can be said about the reactions of Europe's citizens to EU crisis management, although for different reasons in different groups and countries.

The first major set of decisions EU leaders took in their effort to manage the crisis was in 2008 following the collapse of Lehman Brothers in the United States. When it was revealed that European banks, too, had huge toxic assets, EU governments decided to act. Each European government with troubled banks quickly took similar decisions regardless of whether they were within or outside the euro-zone and regardless of whether they had a left- or right-wing government in office. In essence, the decisions amounted to the public sector assuming the responsibility for the private sector's failure, or, to be more specific, for the banking sector's failure. Moreover, although all major banks in trouble operated transnationally, their debts were 'nationalized' and not 'Europeanized'.

This concerted (although not always coordinated) set of decisions had profound implications for the further course of events. First, it exposed different strengths of individual states, especially those within the single currency area. The financial markets subsequently realized that a member state could actually default and they raised the risk premiums on the weaker states with a vengeance. Second, the set of decisions taken put pressure on public expenditures in all states, but especially in the weak ones. Cutting funds for public hospitals, schools and pensions became commonplace, causing enormous social hardship and political contestation. Third, the set of decisions taken directly involved tax-paying citizens in all future European arrangements. A growing conflict was observable between public opinion in the creditor states and in the debtor states, as the former were reluctant to subsidize the latter. For instance, according to the 2013 YouGov poll, some 70 per cent of Germans objected to any suggestion of direct fiscal transfers to euro-zone partners, while 52 per cent opposed any further loans.

The decision that each country should look after its own financial institutions instead of the EU doing it collectively may have been taken on practical grounds, but it broke the principle of solidarity that was one of the bases on which the EU and the euro were based. The decision to bail out banks using public funds was aimed at preventing seemingly imminent economic chaos, but it effectively made those dependent on public provisions 'pay' for the mistakes of the banking sector. This could not but have serious political implications in the long term.

Another major set of decisions taken by EU leaders culminated in the adoption of the so-called 'Fiscal Compact Treaty'. The treaty was signed in March 2012 by all members of the EU, except the Czech Republic and the UK. The Fiscal Compact represents a new, stricter version of the previous Stability and Growth Pact, and runs in parallel with the so-called 'Six Pack'.[8] The treaty introduced several specific provisions such as national 'debt breaks', and a '1/20th rule' that opens countries up to severe sanctions if they do not reduce their excessive debt by 5 per cent a year. However, its symbolic meaning is probably more important than the meaning of its specific provisions. The treaty is seen by many in debtor countries as a symbol of legislating inequality by creditor countries. This is partly because it is largely about punishing weaker states rather than helping them to overcome current problems, since the same strict rules envisaged by the treaty will be more difficult to adhere to for the weak economies than the strong ones. Moreover, it reinforces an austerity policy that is considered unjust and counter-productive by large segments of societies in the weaker countries.

The Fiscal Compact Treaty has also become a symbol of legal and political manipulation. The treaty was launched by the then French President, Nicolas Sarkozy, and the German Chancellor, Angela Merkel, with little consultation with other EU members. In order to avoid a possible veto by some EU member states, the Fiscal Compact was not formally part of the EU treaty framework and it could thus enter into force with only twelve euro-zone members ratifying it. Not surprisingly, the treaty was seen as a means of marginalizing possible dissenters such as the UK. Parliamentarians in creditor member states also pointed out that the treaty undermined their budgetary prerogatives because it obliged governments to follow strict budgetary rules independent of the outcome of parliamentary deliberations. (The same principle seems not to apply to Germany as the German Constitutional Court has already ruled that the decision on revenue and expenditure of the public sector must remain in the hands of the Bundestag.)

In a speech at the signing ceremony of the Fiscal Compact Treaty the President of the European Council, Herman van Rompuy, argued that the treaty would not only reinforce fiscal discipline, but also reinforce trust among member states. It is too early to assess the former, but it is already clear that the treaty has not achieved the latter.

The handling of Cyprus in 2013 may seem like a small episode regarding a small country, but it was also symptomatic of the way the EU responds to crises. In order to minimize the cost of the bailout for creditor countries, the EU (or, to be more specific, the euro-group) insisted on 'bailing in' Cypriot bank depositors (i.e. they were to shoulder some of the costs of their banks' debts). This challenged the business model of European banks, which relies heavily on deposits. If the policy that was tried in Cyprus were to be applied to other countries, this would make weak banks in weaker countries suffer because they would have to pay risk premiums. Small depositors of weak banks in weaker countries would also suffer. Their hard-acquired savings might evaporate overnight, depriving them of essential means of existence. The troubling link between the costs of sovereign debt and bank debt would also be reinforced and with it the gap between the strong and weak states.

Managing the EU's multiple crises was never going to be easy. At the time it unfolded nobody could have grasped the situation in all of its complexity. There were no ready-made solutions for coping with the numerous embodiments of the crisis. EU leaders seemed determined to save the euro, and by extension the EU. However, despite all good intentions, their policies made the EU look stingy, rigid and oppressive. It is now apparent that saving the EU cannot be a low-cost operation, enforcing harsh rules will stir up public protests, and the technocratic mode of governance will help populists prosper. Moreover, the EU's handling of the crises has undermined some long-standing political compromises among member states, with serious constitutional implications. First, a delicate balance between supranationalists and intergovernmentalists within the EU has been tipped in favour of the latter. It is clear that a narrow group of creditor states is now in charge of the EU, with the European Commission playing only a supportive role (i.e. washing the dishes). Second, it is becoming apparent that harsh laws and rules are being drafted with only some EU members in mind, and they will not apply equally to all members. Third, membership of the euro-zone seems to have become more crucial than membership of the EU, and the frontier between these two zones is solidifying. Some states may cross this frontier, as Latvia recently did, but in the future each group will be governed by a different set of laws and rules.

If all these assertions prove correct and lasting, the EU will cease to be a voluntary association of equal states abiding by the rule of law. What will become of it then? And who will be interested in shouldering the costs of its survival? From this rather depressing vantage point, it looks like the EU may well be doomed.

Conclusions

In a world dominated by the media and their quest for spectacle and entertainment, politics is chiefly about crisis. Yet, there are different types of crises, and not all crises are fatal. Some of them can even offer an opportunity for improvement by challenging self-righteousness and prompting a self-reform process. In the past the EU was indeed able to turn crises to its advantage, beefing up its powers and fostering its vision of integration. However, the latest spectacle of confusion, manipulation and incompetence can hardly be transformed in the EU's favour. In this sense it is a wasted crisis. Dramatic events unfolded on various fronts and the behaviour of EU leaders resembled 'the march of folly', to use Barbara Tuchman's expression.[9] Those sitting at the European Council's table ignored all evidence and warnings and generated events that drove them to a place they shouldn't even visit – a place called disintegration.

2

Disintegration

Germany's Chancellor, Angela Merkel, has repeatedly declared that the plunge of the euro would mean the collapse of Europe.[1] In 2011, Poland's then Finance Minister, Jacek Rostowski, added that war could well be the outcome of this scenario.[2] None of this has happened and in the summer of 2013 some analysts began to suggest that the euro-zone's eighteen-month-long recession might be over. Who is right: the pessimists or the optimists? Nobody knows – with the possible exception of a few fortune tellers and astrologers. The Habsburg Empire was said to be mad, bad and unfit to rule, and yet it persisted for over six hundred years. The Soviet Union was said to be remarkably stable, and yet it collapsed with little advance notice, to the embarrassment of Western Kremlin watchers. But are these cases particularly helpful for understanding the rise and fall of the EU, which is said to be *sui generis*? The problem is that EU experts have written a lot about the rise of the EU, but virtually nothing about its possible downfall. We have many theories of European integration, but practically none of European disintegration. It is even difficult to say what disintegration would imply. If Cyprus leaves the euro-zone or the UK successfully renegotiates its terms of EU membership, does this suggest disintegration or merely a legal adjustment? If EU member states vote against each other in the United Nations Security Council, does this denote a routine legitimate disagreement or disintegration? If the euro-zone integrates further, but those EU member states that are unable or unwilling to adopt the euro are left in limbo, is this integration or disintegration? Is disintegration reversible? Is it a product or a process? How much time has to pass before we can conclude whether or not disintegration has actually happened: a month, a year or a decade? And what could be the broader economic, political and international implications of European disintegration? Clearly, it is a struggle to try to address these increasingly pertinent questions.

The problem is compounded by the numerous and fuzzy definitions of integration. Some scholars argue that integration is merely about increased economic and social interactions, but others suggest that it is about building a European super-state. Some see integration as a uni-directional movement from one European treaty to another, but others would like to see a tangible shift of political loyalties to the new European centre before we can talk about it. If we do not really know what integration implies, how can we define the opposite process? And is integration the opposite of disintegration, as democracy is of autocracy? Can the single market project progress despite the fall of the single currency or disintegration in the field of Justice and Home Affairs? Can the 'North Sea Alliance' integrate while 'Club Med' is disintegrating? There is no point in multiplying these kinds of tortuous questions, yet we need to search for a minimum degree of intellectual clarity or else face onerous practical consequences.

At least three possible scenarios of disintegration require scrutiny. The first sees Europe's leaders losing control over the unfolding financial or political events. The second suggests that they try to address problems, but end up making things worse. The third scenario envisages a benign-neglect policy with not so benign implications. As Ivan Krastev suggested: 'The EU's disintegration need not be the result of a victory by anti-EU forces over pro-EU forces. If it happens, it will probably be an unintended consequence of the Union's paralysis, compounded by the elites' misreading of national political dynamics.'[3]

Scenarios of disintegration

At the peak of the euro crisis, an economic avalanche beyond anybody's control was seen as the most likely scenario of disintegration. The term 'avalanche', rather than 'tsunami', suggests that disintegration could be man-made: for instance, by pushing Greece out of the euro-zone. In 2012 such a step may have sounded like a reasonable response to public opinion in Germany, France or Holland, but policy-makers clearly feared that it could prompt an unmanageable sequence of events. At the time, some analysts predicted that the Greek exit, or 'Grexit' as it was called in financial circles, could trigger a 50 per cent fall in euro stocks, while others estimated the costs of the Greek default to be similar to those inflicted by the Lehman Brothers failure. Mutual accusations, retaliations and recriminations would surely follow such disastrous economic developments, generating political chaos. Germany would be the prime suspect in the ensuing blame game. Some countries would create a band-wagon behind Germany; others would try to form a counter-alliance to balance it. Since chaos is heaven for populist politics, nationalism would thrive. The politics of territorial claims and financial recrimina-tions would ensue. Some argued that the end result would be the rise of the Fourth Reich, while others predicted a return to Westphalia. Needless to say, Ms Merkel was very keen to avoid either scenario, but some of her country's politicians were happy to endorse the 'Grexit', nevertheless. Luckily for Merkel, the German Constitutional Court stopped short of judging the Greek bailout unconstitutional, and her cautious policy prevailed.

Each time the financial markets stopped hammer-ing the euro, the abrupt scenario of disintegration seemed less credible. However, it is too early to say that the euro is safe and well. A 2013 study of pos-sible scenarios for the euro-zone in the year 2020 prepared by the Friedrich-Ebert-Stiftung still argues that the 'euro house' can fall apart.[4] Moreover, the EU may again find itself in trouble owing to the pressure of external shocks that have little to do with the euro as such. Consider, for instance, the economic implications for Europe of a possible crisis in China. China is by far the EU's biggest source of imports, and has also become one of its fastest growing export markets. The EU has also become China's biggest source of imports. China and Europe now trade well over €1 billion a day. China also has large holdings of the euro. The situation in Europe's backyards, from Tripoli and Cairo to Pristina, Minsk and Kiev, is also not comforting. A cocktail of internal and external shocks can produce a spiral of events that would be beyond anybody's control. Europe's leaders have numerous instruments to cope with economic and political shocks, but it is naïve to think that they are always able to steer the rapidly evolving course of events. Besides, regardless of intentions, their policies may make the situation worse rather than better.

Reforms may sometimes spark dramatic unintended outcomes, which brings us to another possible scenario of disintegration. The Soviet Union collapsed after Mikhail Gorbachev began introducing economic and democratic reforms. Historians point to reforms of the Habsburg Empire that accelerated its demise. The so-called 'Austro-Hungarian Compromise' of 1867, which led to the creation of a dual monarchy with two separate parliaments and prime ministers in Budapest and Vienna, provides a good example. At present the 2012 Fiscal Compact is said to be driving the Union apart because it imposes excessively rigid, counter-productive policies on the debtor states which some have also considered unjust. Plans to create a more ambitious economic and political union as a response to the euro crisis could have even more profound negative implications.

A political and economic union of many distinct entities, however interdependent, would be at pains to identify a set of common interests that could guide its policies. It would only work if composed of a few like-minded and similar-looking European states. Such a core Europe would create a new divide across the continent, raising fear and suspicion. Some EU member states would be worried about being excluded, while others would fear that joining would subject them to domination by other core members. In other words, a jump into a fully fledged union is likely to destabilize relations among European states, and break cooperative arrangements. A federation, however light, may well be attempted with the intention of saving integration, but in reality it may well prompt disintegration.

Disintegration may also be caused by the reforms to the EU advocated by the UK under David Cameron. The official aim of the proposed reforms is certainly noble: making the EU more flexible, competitive, and taking account of the changes within the euro-zone. This is why Cameron can rely on the support of several EU partners who have become impatient with Brussels' rigidity and immobility. However, the form of orchestrating the reforms through the process of renegotiating the existing treaties is likely to generate conflicts and diplomatic deadlocks. Cameron himself contemplates not merely universal reforms, but also specific UK opt-outs from EU employment law, social policies, criminal law and regional funding structures. Cameron's allies will all have different individual opt-outs in mind as well, and it is far from certain that they will agree on the overall blueprint of universal reforms. The fact that the outcome of treaty renegotiations is subject to national referenda in some countries leaves little room for pragmatic solutions. Moreover, repatriation of certain powers from Brussels to national capitals and the reduction of budgetary contributions to the EU is not likely to revitalize the integration project; rather the reverse. After all, openly anti-European parties such as UKIP, the True Finns or the Dutch Party for Freedom advocate similar budgetary cuts and repatriation of powers from Brussels.

In view of this analysis one wonders whether changing little or nothing is not a wiser policy in this uncertain period of European history. This leads to the benign-neglect or muddling-through scenario. This scenario may lead to disintegration on the assumption that muddling through also comes at a price, and that benign neglect is a synonym for blind neglect or even malign neglect.

Under the benign-neglect scenario, disintegration will take place by default or in disguise. Rather than trying to look for European solutions to national problems, member states will increasingly try to solve problems on their own or within a non-European framework. They will not openly abandon the European project, but use it merely as a public relations tool. The long history of the Western European Union (WEU) is a good example of such a symbolic cooperative frame. The WEU existed for many decades, but was hardly ever utilized for its envisaged security purposes. Members of the WEU met regularly and adopted resolutions. The WEU administrative structure and even the parliamentary assembly functioned seemingly normally. And yet, when serious challenges arose in the field of defence and security, the WEU member states ignored the WEU structure and used the NATO, EU, UN, OSCE or some informal frameworks instead. The war in the Balkans uncovered the price of this policy. Europeans found themselves without a common security strategy, divided on the question of which institution should handle the war, and with no effective military capabilities to do anything meaningful.

A policy of muddling through and benign neglect has its costs, but it is better than endorsing highly ambitious, hazardous projects. In a period of economic turmoil and ideological confusion, pragmatism is a valid alternative to idealism; a gradual approach may work better than a revolutionary one. This probably explains the policy of European leaders at present. They are clearly reluctant to invest their careers and resources in policies with highly uncertain outcomes. They do the minimum to avert a financial meltdown and political confrontation, but not enough to halt the process of creeping disintegration. The EU is the obvious victim of such an approach, with some of its key institutions progressively marginalized. However, institutions have a very long half-life, even when they are not working, which suggests that the EU, or rather its façade, will survive. Europe will increasingly resemble a maze with different actors moving in opposite directions, whilst maintaining the appearance of dialogue and cooperation. To reverse the famous Lampedusan dictum: trying to change nothing may result in changing everything.

Engines of disintegration

The envisaged scenarios suggest that integration and disintegration are not necessarily products of deliberate decisions. They are both processes set in motion by responses to internal and external trends and shocks. These responses are guided by a variety of both officially stated and disguised motivations; they generate both intended and unintended consequences. Many more actors than just the twenty-eight EU member states have some impact here. External powers, EU institutions, cities and regions, transnational markets and something that is vaguely called civil society – they all play their part in the on-going European spectacle. They all have diversified interests, informed by a variety of values. In the final analysis, however, they are faced with a straightforward question: is integration good for them? If the answer is negative or ambivalent, they are not likely to endorse the costs involved in repairing and saving the EU. The EU has promised many good things, but it has failed to deliver on some of them. Those unfulfilled promises represent the true engines of disintegration. They suggest that the EU is increasingly set to fail, despite official denial.

European integration was, first of all, supposed to

get rid of power politics. Large and rich states were no longer to bully small and impoverished ones. Above all, Europe was not to be ruled by Germany. Today a few 'triple A' countries run Europe with Germany in the driving seat. Gone is equality among member states. New treaties are written with only some states in mind; external (arbitrary) interference in domestic affairs abounds; and policies are chiefly about punishment rather than help and incentives.

European integration was also supposed to create the most competitive economy in the world. It was, moreover, intended to make the 'Stockholm consensus' prevail over the 'Washington consensus', not just in the north, but also in the east and south of Europe. The common currency and the single market were the key means for achieving these ambitious economic aims. Today the common currency is in trouble and it undermines the achievements of the single market. Even the strongest European economies fail to generate growth and Europe's welfare systems are collapsing. The euro was meant to help integrate Europe, but it achieved the opposite: it exacerbated the gaps and conflicts between the surplus and deficit countries, the importers and exporters, and the north and south.

European integration was more about efficiency than citizens' participation, yet it never questioned the principles of democracy. Today some key decisions are being made by the ECB, the IMF and the German Constitutional Court with only symbolic input from the European Council representing democratically elected leaders. Citizens in individual states are free to elect their governments, but these governments are not free to change the course of their policies. The powers of the European Parliament (EP) have been progressively augmented, but fewer and fewer people bother to vote in European elections, and an ever-larger percentage of elected European MPs is euro-sceptic. The strength of the EP as an institution has been achieved at the expense of its representative role.

European decision-making was always terribly complex, slow and hostage to the lowest common denominator. Yet today the problem seems to be a much more fundamental one. European institutions look disconnected from both national politics and global markets. They seem to operate in a political and economic vacuum unable to make any significant impact on either citizens or firms. Adjusting EU laws to ever-changing realities has become problematic, and the compliance record is disappointing.

The EU used to be an influential international actor despite its largely civilian nature. Its policy of enlargement generated security and prosperity in post-communist Eastern Europe. EU regulatory regimes imposed extra-territorial scrutiny on numerous trading partners across the world. Today, however, the EU no longer generates security, but instead instils insecurity. Further enlargements have been put on hold, Europeans clash in the UN Security Council, and the European External Action Service cannot get off the ground. The EU fails to steer global trade or environmental negotiations, leaving its citizens exposed to global turbulence.

The EU was said to be a master of institutional engineering with no ambition to create a distinct 'imagined community'. Its case rested on the modernist notion of competence and progress rather than traditional notions of loyalty, trust or affection. The crisis has undermined the EU's modernist credentials and has exasperated conflicts between Europe's nations and peoples. Today 'unity in diversity' seems to be an empty slogan and the EU lacks a recognizable 'self' that would make people stick to the Union in these difficult times.

Dynamics of disintegration

Assessing the dynamics of integration is always tricky because different actors have different

interests and perceptions. What represents pro-
gress in integration for some is regress for others.
Moreover, EU policy failures need not signify disin-
tegration, but may herald the reverse. For instance,
Europe's inability to properly address the Balkan
war prompted France and the UK to create the St
Malo framework for Europe's common defence.
Likewise, failure properly to address the threat of
Muslim extremism epitomized by the Madrid and
London bombings (and of course by 9/11) provided
Europe with an impulse for closer integration in the
field of Justice and Home Affairs. In other words,
structural prerequisites for disintegration do not
need to cause actual disintegration. Disintegration
is only likely to evolve under the pressure of a
certain combination of events. Can we detect such
dynamics of disintegration at present?

Two factors seem particularly striking. First,
the EU has yet to develop an effective mechanism
to manage the three distinct domains – economic,
political and institutional – in which the European
crisis is being played out. These domains or theatres
take up different spaces, feature different actors and
work according to different logics, and the policies
evolving in each of them undermine rather than
support one another. The European case illustrates
how hard it is to conduct public affairs beyond the

nation state. But efforts to transform the EU into a stronger federation are highly contentious and, as pointed out earlier, may reinforce rather than stop disintegration.

Second, the EU lacks sound democratic means to legitimate its policies. Policies decided upon during a time of crisis are bound to be controversial, and yet will need to quell the anxieties of diverse publics across the vast European space. The EU's legitimacy rests primarily on efficiency, not democracy or national identity. When its institutions become inefficient, the EU loses its main reason for being.

The EU crisis is like a war being fought in distinct but related theatres – land, air and sea – in which different actors set the agenda according to different logics.[5] The relative importance of the different theatres changes over time, but the final outcome depends on the commanders' ability to manage all three theatres in conjunction with one another. Put differently, Europe's leaders need to combat the crisis simultaneously in the domain of global economics, national politics and European institutions. To control financial and political markets they cannot just apply the means suited for the institutional theatre.

The key actors in the economic theatre are bankers, traders, producers, consumers and investors.

They are usually private, but also include public actors such as states, which are major regulators, owners and investors. EU institutions fill supporting roles, trying to raise and maintain the markets' confidence (albeit with mixed results at best so far). The economic theatre is global, which explains why EU institutions only play a limited part. Of course, the EU is an important global actor: it generates a quarter of the world's GNP, is responsible for about two-fifths of the world's exports, and the euro remains the second-largest global currency. However, much of the European economy comprises a complex set of economic activities that are outside of the control of the European Council and the ECB. None of the highly ambitious European projects, such as the single market, the single currency or the development plan set forth in the Lisbon Agenda, have been able to generate impressive rates of economic growth or secure economic convergence between Europe's more and less affluent economies.

Much of Europe's ostensible wealth came from excessive borrowing – hence the austerity policy demanded by creditor countries such as Austria, Finland, Germany, Luxembourg and the Netherlands. But austerity is hampering, rather than promoting, economic growth in countries such as Greece, Ireland, Italy, Portugal and Spain. EU attempts to rescue individual banks and states also have failed to impress the markets. Economists argue that a monetary union requires a fiscal and banking union. But such a union would mean that creditor states would have to send money to debtor states, without a firm system of controls and limits. Moreover, it would be a step towards deeper political integration, something that voters in creditor states broadly oppose. And so we enter the political theatre.

The political theatre revolves around elections which are being contested separately in all twenty-eight distinct EU polities. While elections to the EP have a pan-European character, votes are cast separately in each member state, with national rather than European issues dominating the campaigns. The outcomes of national elections, meanwhile, often have Europe-wide implications, and thus external actors sometimes seek to influence them. However, the political theatre of each member state has its own idiosyncrasies: communication is exclusively in the national language; the rules of combat reflect distinct cultural patterns; victorious commanders may look like 'heroes' within local communities but rarely outside them. It is hard to explain the electoral appeal of Silvio Berlusconi to non-Italians. Hardly anybody outside their respective countries knows the names of leading Finnish, Austrian or Slovenian politicians unless they are implicated in a huge international scandal.

The political theatre generates policies driven by national interests, justified in part by different national circumstances: Germany's economy, with its myriad small and medium-sized export-based enterprises, needs different policies from the UK's service-based economy with its strong financial sector. The source of Spain's woes was a property bubble, whereas in Italy it was the oversized and inefficient public sector. National egos and prejudices have also played a part – leading to disputes between the EU 'colonels' and 'field soldiers', 'insiders' and 'outsiders', those contributing to the EU budget and those benefiting from it, and pitting 'lazy' southern states against 'despotic' northern ones, and "sinful" Catholic regions against "rigid" Protestant ones. In an atmosphere of distrust and mutual accusations, there is little space for pan-European solidarity.

The institutional theatre is uniquely European. The EU Council plays the leading role, but the ECB, EP, European Commission and European Court of Justice have their parts too. The main concern in this theatre is governance – the making and implementing of rules. Historically, implementation has been left to national governments, hence the recent squabbles between creditor and debtor states over enforcement procedures and sanctions. European laws, however, are anything but straightforward.

The Lisbon Treaty, signed by the EU member states in 2007 after the failed attempt to approve a 'constitutional' treaty, is an awkward and anachronistic compilation of earlier treaties. It disperses authority to various governmental centres that often have different geographical reaches and operate in different functional fields. Major pillars of European integration, such as the single market, the single currency and the Schengen (open-borders) area, have different members and rules. As a result, the EU decision-making system is very slow and complex, which explains why major powers tend to become impatient and impose their will on lesser ones in the European Council.

The EU has considerable economic power, but political power rests chiefly with the member states. The crisis has exacerbated the flaws of an integration process that has narrowed the space for political decisions at the national level without widening it at the European level. On the one hand, the EU demands austerity, bans central-bank interventions,

prevents parliaments from taking sovereign decisions and ejects democratically elected politicians.
On the other hand, it does not protect against
unregulated markets, socialize debt or allow citizens to shape EU-level decisions. Finally, while
most national leaders agree that the survival of the
euro-zone depends upon deeper integration, they
cannot agree on how to move forward. And there is
little enthusiasm for a federative project among the
European public, raising the question of democratic
legitimacy.

Legitimizing a frail project

The European project has always relied on output
rather than input legitimacy, which means that
efficiency, not democracy, has been its key rationale. The EU has stimulated economic growth
and created institutional channels of cooperation
(bargaining) among former enemies. By lowering
barriers to the movement of goods, labour, services
and people, integration has also aided the growth of
a European cultural and political identity. The key
goal has been to make Europe more prosperous,
on the assumption that this by itself will generate public support or at least a 'permissive public

consensus' for the integration project. EU efforts to involve ordinary citizens in its work, however, have been sporadic, heavy-handed and artificial.

The EU is run by a narrow group of elites with little involvement from citizens, who must accede to ever-changing arrangements without an opportunity to deliberate over their scope and shape. National parliaments ratifying European treaties cannot unravel the results of complex intergovernmental negotiations. If a country such as Ireland or Denmark votes 'no' in a referendum on a European treaty, its people are made to vote again after small concessions and huge external pressures are brought to bear to make them change their minds.

It is not that the EU has ignored democracy entirely. Members of the European Council represent democratically elected governments, and they maintain veto rights over many matters important to their citizens. The powers of the EP have also gradually expanded, offering citizens some standard means of contestation. They can petition the EP and appeal to the European Ombudsman with complaints about most EU institutions. Individuals also have the right to access EU documents and to petition EU institutions and receive a reply. However, none of these measures afford the EU any sound input legitimacy. Few people bother voting in EP elections, and large numbers of those who do cast ballots do so in order to endorse anti-European politicians. French and Dutch voters struck down a draft of the European Constitution in referendums in their respective countries. (Similar negative results could be expected in some other countries had a referendum been held.) Nor are there any significant civil society movements campaigning at the grassroots for greater European integration.

In recent years EU member states have been criticized for failing to offer their citizens sufficient means of participation, representation and accountability. How can we expect the EU to do any better? Brussels is naturally more detached from the concerns of, say, Danish citizens than is Copenhagen, and Danish voters obviously have less opportunity to influence the complex governance machinery in Brussels. Securing citizens' participation in a huge multilevel polity like the EU was never going to be easy; parliamentary representation in a polity comprising twenty-eight distinct *demoi* can hardly work well; and accountability is difficult in a complex institutional context with blurred lines of responsibility. Nevertheless, the EU has acquired significant powers, and the use of these powers has to be legitimated.

The crisis has tested the assumption that the EU

and the euro-zone in particular are in a strong position to deal with global financial turbulence, thus undermining the EU's output-based legitimacy. At the same time, the crisis has exposed the weakness of input-based legitimacy. Measures such as debt mutualization via some form of euro-zone bonds, demanded by financial markets, amount to major resource transfers from creditor to debtor states. Such transfers need the backing of creditor-state voters, who mostly feel reluctant – especially if the transfers are not tied to tough austerity and monitoring measures in debtor countries.

Creditor states have bluntly told debtor-state electorates that there is no alternative to harsh austerity and painful structural reforms: they can change their governments, but not the austerity policies imposed by their stronger European partners. This has generated a backlash in some of the troubled states, where radical anti-establishment parties campaigning against the EU have made considerable electoral gains and press mainstream pro-European parties to reverse the course. In short, the electorates in both creditor and debtor states are profoundly disenchanted with demands coming from Europe.

The EU's institutions offer procedural channels for pan-European decision-making, but lack channels for pan-European public deliberation and political bargaining. As the crisis worsened, it became clear that the integration project was developing common policy-making without common politics. In the EU, technocrats dominate policy-making while populists dominate politics. Technocrats from different countries remain divided, while populists are fairly united. Ideologically, the left-wing Greek Syriza and the right-wing Dutch Freedom Party are seas apart, but both campaign on the same slogan of taking power from Brussels and bringing it back home. Likewise, in Italy parties from both the extreme left and the extreme right oppose EU-imposed policies and complain of 'suspended democracy' in their country.

This technocratic–populist trap has prompted discussions about the need to create a fully fledged political union – a federation that would rely on tested democratic devices to legitimate policies of austerity and transfers. But will publics support giving more power to Europe at a time when Europe is performing so badly?

Conclusions

Integration can be understood as a response to cascading interdependence. Europeans are increasingly linked to each other, and it makes obvious sense to pool resources to tackle common challenges. Moreover, in the first decades of European integration, cooperation in one field exerted pressure to extend cooperation to another, again because of interconnections between various fields across state borders. For instance, the initial integration of the steel and coal sectors could not progress properly without integrating the transport sector among member states. The decision to create a free trade area generated pressures for creating a customs union, a common market and a common currency. This process has been labelled a functional spill-over, and it largely explains how we moved from the Coal and Steel Community to the European Economic Communities and to the European Union. Of course, the spill-over did not evolve automatically without political decisions and institutional engineering. It is also clear that it has not been even across all fields. Economic integration progressed much more smoothly than political integration. However, interdependence seemed to generate integration of numerous policy fields and made the EU increasingly responsible for running them.

Moreover, interdependence generated not only functional, but also territorial spill-over. Extending tested forms of integration to other European countries became the norm. The EU has enlarged several times in its history, from the original six to twenty-eight members, the latest 'acquisition' being Croatia in 2013. This was not only to take advantage of economic scale, but also to handle interdependence in the field of security, migration and the environment. The official policy always was that the widening of the EU should go hand in hand with its deepening. The same rules applied to all members with only a few small and usually temporary exceptions. The process was described as a win-win game for all parties involved.

Today, this process seems to be reversed. It looks as though the pendulum of interdependence has swung over: interdependence no longer generates integration but instead prompts disintegration. We observe a negative spill-back process instead of a positive spill-over one, meaning that disintegration in one field prompts disintegration in another. Sebastian Dullien has analysed the three most likely scenarios for how the euro crisis is likely to develop, and showed that each would adversely affect the single market and harm cross-border business and travel within the EU.[6] A full break-up of the euro-zone would lead to huge macro-economic disruptions manifested by a large drop in economic activity, a strong increase in unemployment and widespread bank failures. The Schengen agreement on free travel would also be threatened under this scenario, affecting numerous cross-border networks that have been important not only in increasing the efficiency and competitiveness of the European manufacturing sector, but also in spreading techno-logical progress. In a muddling-through scenario, economic growth would remain subdued in the euro-zone over years and the euro periphery would experience only a very slow and sluggish recovery from its recession. A 'positive' solution to the crisis in the euro-zone, involving a great leap towards a true fiscal and banking union, would probably see several countries (such as the UK) withdraw, shrinking the single market.

Political implications of such scenarios are likely to be devastating. The euro crisis has already undermined mutual trust across the continent and marginalized European institutions. There are clear winners and losers emerging from the crisis. Efforts to halt disintegration are about creating more 'Europes' and not more Europe, meaning a single integrated continent. In this case politics has fol-lowed economics, but in a negative sense. The question is: will this trend be allowed to progress?

3

Reintegration

In 2013 some of Europe's leading newspapers asked six of their senior journalists to suggest ideas to save the EU.[1] Some of the proposed ideas were useful, but too modest to make the EU significantly more efficient and popular. For instance, Ian Traynor from the *Guardian* suggested stopping the shuttling of Members of the European Parliament between the Parliament's two sites in Strasbourg and Brussels. The suggestion was perfectly sensible but hardly likely to reverse the EU's fortunes. Other ideas proposed were more ambitious and comprehensive: Philippe Ricard from *Le Monde* called for the creation of a European army and Claudi Pérez of *El País* suggested creating a new European democracy. Both, however, seemed well aware that their proposals are virtually impossible to realize at the present time. Ricard acknowledged that a rapprochement of the European Aeronautic Defence and Space Company (EADS) and the British aerospace and defence company BAE Systems to create a European defence and aviation giant had just been vetoed by Chancellor Merkel. Pérez could not envisage what a new European division of power and competences should actually look like. Saving the EU is clearly a formidable challenge. But what is the rationale for saving it? Does the EU still perform useful functions, and can one envisage integration without the EU?

Defending the EU

These days it is hard to find a European policy-maker genuinely enthusiastic about the EU. I have spoken to many 'off the record', and I have been stunned by their scepticism. Politicians across Europe read opinion polls which tell them that campaigning for the EU will not result in electoral gains, and may even cost votes in some cases. Civil servants are frustrated by the EU's complex decision-making system and lack of viable enforcement capacities. Policy-makers in creditor states complain that keeping the EU on life support is costing them money with no clear prospect of the 'patient's' recovery. Adopting any new rules within the EU is extremely cumbersome, and the results of complex intergovernmental negotiations usually fail to reflect the paymasters' priorities. Even if the creditors get the laws they wish, these laws are hardly ever implemented by the debtor states, which are suspected of cheating. Policy-makers in the debtor states, for their part, complain that they are faced with unjust, arbitrary and unworkable conditions from Brussels. They see the EU as an instrument of the most powerful states with few resources to address their needs and little cross-border solidarity.

If those in charge of running the EU are so Euro-sceptical, how is it that the EU still exists? Why do Europe's policy-makers bash the EU in private but defend it in public? Are they simply hypocritical? Or are they unable to invent a workable alternative? The EU has failed to live up to some key expectations, but this does not mean that it has achieved nothing positive and significant. Dismantling of the EU may undo accomplishments of European integration, and leave member states with no '*ready-made*' instruments to cope with mounting economic or even security challenges. How many of us have been keeping an old, uncomfortable, fuel-thirsty and malfunctioning car because a new car is too expensive and public transport is highly unreliable?

Repairing an old dysfunctional car may seem a more rational solution than getting rid of it, provided that the repairs do not cost too much. Similar reasoning may apply to the EU, but, of course, the stakes involved are much more serious. European politics is not just about moving from one place to another. It is also, if not chiefly, about peace and prosperity. Even passionate Euro-sceptics acknowledge some of the accomplishments of European integration in this respect, and so far this integration has been symbolized by the EU.

To begin with, the EU may not be the sole factor behind the six decades of peace among former enemies, but to ignore the role of economic integration in promoting political reconciliation would be a misreading of history. It is quite legitimate to worry that the possible economic disintegration will generate political conflicts of some sorts. Economic disintegration may also jeopardize Europe's economic prosperity. According to Hans-Werner Sinn's calculations, should Greece, Ireland, Italy, Portugal and Spain go bankrupt and repay nothing, while the euro survives, Germany would lose $899 billion. Should the euro fail, Germany would lose over $1.35 trillion, more than 40 per cent of its GDP.[2]

The EU may have done many silly things such as trying to define the proper shape of a banana.

However, it has also done numerous virtuous things, which have helped Europe's citizens to achieve remarkable wealth by any comparative global standard. The EU worked hard to abolish barriers to the movement of capital, goods, services and people within its borders. It created and enforced rules of economic competition. It negotiated external trade agreements on behalf of all its members. It helped weaker economic actors (such as farmers in the private sector and regions in the public sector) to cope with economic pressures. It opened and transformed the markets of neighbouring countries through its policy of conditional accession to the EU or through various forms of association. True, most of Europe's economies have not been growing for some time now and some are in recession at present. However, many different factors contributed to Europe's economic stagnation, and it would be unfair to blame the EU for Europe's demography or consumption habits. Above all, it is hard to blame the EU for an ever-more competitive China or an ever-more assertive Russia under the presidency of Vladimir Putin.

Another important reason for keeping the EU alive relates to international competition. The EU helps its member states, most of them small or medium-size, to punch above their weight in the world of global rivalry dominated by such rising giants as China, Russia, India, Brazil or Indonesia. Fierce competition from formal allies such as the United States or Japan should also be reckoned with. There is a difference when trade agreements with these giants are negotiated by the EU rather than by individual member states. At stake are not only economic profits, but also basic European social values. Aggregated trade leverage helps the EU to promote global regulatory standards that make it possible for Europeans to enjoy certain social rights or environmental standards. The EU has also helped Europeans to face corporate global giants. Consider, for instance, the mega fine of $1.4bn imposed on Microsoft for its failure to comply with European regulatory demands to end anti-competitive business practices. Or think about the European Court's decision effectively to prohibit the merger of two US companies, General Motors and Honeywell Bull. This added value of the EU cannot be ignored even by Germany or the UK, let alone by tiny Malta or Latvia.

The above rational arguments are probably sufficient for understanding policy-makers' reluctance to give up on the EU despite all of its deficiencies. However, irrational arguments should also be taken into consideration. Some policy-makers cultivate nostalgia for the European 'dream', however illusory it may seem at present. They have spent a large part of their professional careers within the European framework. The EU framework has become the most crucial centre of European policy debates, where national policies meet and part. Collective bargaining over laws, procedures and the Union's institutional structure has become the daily routine of Europe's policy-makers. They are used to speaking and acting 'in the name of Europe', if not through Europe itself. This is particularly pronounced in Germany, but also in Italy, Spain or Poland, where policy-makers refer to the EU as a matter of course with little effort to bridge their pro-European rhetoric with not so pro-European policies. For instance, they often want Europe to be in charge of certain issues, but refuse to grant the EU the required financial resources for undertaking new tasks.

Symbolic attachment aside, there is also the fear of the unknown. What could the demise of the EU bring about? The most paralysing thought is not just the fear of known unknowns, such as the need to construct a new legal framework of European cooperation in case the EU is formally dissolved. Much more paralysing is the fear of unknown unknowns, to use a famous phrase coined by the infamous

Donald Rumsfeld. The latter are by their nature highly speculative and irrational, but they are also the most apocalyptic. The fear of chaos and possibly war features prominently among the unknown unknowns. I will return to this fear in the next chapter. For now it is enough to conclude that the EU will not be abandoned, for a variety of rational and irrational calculations. The EU still performs some important functions, and policy-makers fear the possible implications of disintegration, those known and unknown. The question is whether it can be repaired.

A United States of Europe

Critics of Europe's Economic and Monetary Union (EMU) have always argued that it created a house half-built: a common currency without a common economic government. The obvious solution therefore seems to be the completion of the European construction. However, putting the EU in charge of economic supervision, taxation, redistribution and social welfare would imply a major transfer of sovereignty from member states to Brussels. Will member states agree to that? Moreover, an EU in charge of such major economic policies would need to have stronger democratic legitimacy. To quote the famous saying dating back to the American War of Independence: 'no taxation without representation'. Can the EU offer such representation? In other words, can there be a functioning fiscal and economic union without a plausible political union? Some policy-makers believe that one cannot function properly without the other and argue for a major leap towards political union; others are less sure about or even hostile towards the idea. For instance, the President of the European Commission, José Manuel Barroso, in his 2011 speech to the European Parliament, called for 'a new federalizing moment' that would generate 'deeper and more results-driven integration', based on the Community method rather than intergovernmental cooperation.[3] Chancellor Merkel in her 2010 speech at the College of Europe in Bruges endorsed the Union method: 'coordinated action in a spirit of solidarity – each of us [i.e. member states] in the area for which we are responsible but all working towards the same goal'.[4] The UK's Prime Minister, David Cameron, in his 2013 speech at Bloomberg insisted that 'power must be able to flow back to Member States, not just away from them', and he argued that the EU should abandon the commitment to 'ever-closer union' included in its founding treaty.[5]

Clearly, no agreement on the political union is in sight. The major points of contention concern five fundamental questions. How much sovereignty, if any, could be transferred from the national to the European level? Does the EU need strict common rules, or a strong European government, or both? Will centralization of power result in greater efficiency, let alone legitimacy? Should transfer of powers concern only members of the euro-zone, and if so, what are the implications for other members of the EU? Will measures adopted in defence of the euro strengthen or weaken the single market, Schengen and the Common Foreign and Security Policy (CFSP)? Different answers to these questions have numerous practical implications. At stake is not just the future institutional architecture, but the power of various political actors and the prosperity of Europe's citizens.

Sovereignty has a less absolute meaning for economists and political scientists than for lawyers. The former will suggest that nation-states' power has been progressively eroded for a long time now by what we call globalization, and European integration was a means for regaining some political control over transnational capital flows, migration, services and crime. Sceptics may well argue that European integration has increased system effectiveness only modestly, while eroding citizens' participation quite substantially. But their arguments become less credible when they insist that individual European states with their democratic parliaments are in a better position to cope with global pressures than the EU as such. Sovereignty is a meaningful concept only when a state's legal-political borders overlap with its market transaction fringes, military frontiers and migration traits. This has not been the case for quite a while.

However, delegating sovereignty to the European level curbs the power of national institutions and they are the gatekeepers of the EU and integration at present. The French President, the German Chancellor and the Dutch Prime Minister understand the force of transnational capital markets and migratory pressures, but they do not want to be outvoted in the European Council on crucial matters. National parliaments are also unhappy about delegating their powers to the European Parliament, which is less representative than they are by any available measure. The same applies to central banks and courts. In numerous member states they are independent veto players able to block European legislation. Even if laws are adopted, implementation of these laws is subject to compliance of these national players. For instance, the envisaged EU banking union gives the ECB sweeping legal powers to supervise and regulate some 6,000 euro-zone banks. However, it remains to be seen whether national banks will agree to function only as reporting agencies, devoid of all power to regulate and supervise their own banking sectors.

National gatekeepers' reluctance to cede powers explains why, in the process of European integration, we observed more progress in common rule-making than in empowering central European government. Europe's responses to the crisis reinforced this trend. The Fiscal Compact Treaty obliged member states to change their national constitutions to introduce debt-brake provisions and accept monitoring and sanctions by the European Court of Justice should they fail to comply with the new provisions. However, the treaty did not create a European economic government in charge of member states' fiscal and economic policies. The body envisaged by the treaty and its President are in a position to oversee the implementation of the agreed rules, but they cannot provide day-to-day governance. In fact, strict rules stipulated by the treaty make it difficult to practise any governance because they reduce discretionary powers of political and economic actors at local, national and

European levels. Nor is it evident that a federal path will increase Europe's cohesion and effectiveness.

Economists often argue that policies should respond to ever-changing circumstances and that they cannot just follow general rules. Moreover, current rules are being criticized for their excessive rigidity and inability to reflect the different economic circumstances of individual member states. Can one credibly argue that one set of rules will fit countries as diverse as France, Cyprus, Austria or Estonia? In addition, excessive harmonization and centralization hamper competition, which is the engine of economic progress and growth. In other words, steps towards economic and political union may not necessarily make Europe more efficient. At the same time, they are producing economic and political winners and losers. The Fiscal Compact and other measures adopted during the crisis have already been criticized for reflecting the preferences of creditor states and their banks. This is an important reason why policy-makers are hesitant to jump on the supranational 'train'.

Another dispute concerns the composition of an economic and political union. A major leap towards such a union is currently contemplated only within the euro-zone, but this leaves several EU members outside the scheme. Some are unable to join the euro-zone, while others are unwilling to do so, but they all are directly affected by developments within it. They obviously want to be policy-makers and not just policy-takers within the EU and do not cherish the prospect of having a second- or even third-rank membership. It is virtually impossible to find an arrangement that would please all current EU members. Possible arrangements are also problematic from a practical point of view. For instance, does it make sense for a fiscal union to exclude the major European banking centre: London's City? Can federal economic governance apply only to some parts of the single market?

A further major dilemma confronts the prospect of economic and political union. Such a union can presumably only work well for a few countries of like mind and like characteristics. However, excluding several current EU members from the federal scheme may well result in disintegration rather than integration. Put differently, efforts to save the euro may well damage other integrative arrangements such as the single market, Schengen or Europe's CFSP. One can hardly talk about integration if some EU member states are left in the cold.

In the past it was often assumed that the creation of the euro would pave the way to a United States of Europe. Today the latter project is being contemplated as a means to save the euro. However, it is not likely to materialize for a number of reasons already mentioned. Compromise or half-baked solutions will not make things better. José Ignacio Torreblanca and Sebastian Dullien analysed different options for the creation of an economic and political union in depth and they concluded that a pick and mix approach is unsustainable.[6] The Union may end up with all the negative rather than positive aspects of the various solutions, namely an economic and political union that is inefficient and seen as illegitimate. The result may be another economic and political crisis.

Bundesrepublik *Europa*

If a United States of Europe is not a viable option, can reintegration be attempted through the construction of a Federal Republic of Europe with Berlin rather than Brussels as its key centre?[7] Germany is by far the most powerful country on the continent, it has ample experience in federation building, and its policies have been closely aligned with Europe for the last six decades. During the crisis Germany has emerged as Europe's leader, able to build coalitions with other states to push through policies prepared in Berlin. Germany is also the country with the most to lose if chaos and conflict spread across the continent. It trades more within the EU than other member states, and it borders more states than any other EU member.

If the EU were to collapse, Germany would find itself in the middle of the ensuing geopolitical earthquake. Envoys from European states would rush to Berlin in search of economic help, diplomatic mediation and even German intervention to deal with their domestic 'trouble-makers'. The breakdown of the euro would spur several countries to tie their national currencies to the German mark, and this would only reinforce Germany's dominant economic position. Even artists would begin to travel en masse to Berlin, Dresden and Frankfurt in search of inspiration and patronage. Germany would become a new imperial centre as a result.

There are good reasons to believe that a new German empire will be considerate, restrained and benign. Since World War II, Germany has showed no intention whatsoever of returning to the path of military adventurism. Germany is now a stable and democratic country which sees itself as a civilian rather than military power. In fact, it has often been criticized for pacifism and introversion in international politics, especially by American, British or

French commentators. Moreover, Germany did not seek the leadership position in Europe it found itself in. As the crisis erupted, Germany was not only the largest, but also one of the healthiest economic actors following painful reforms in the aftermath of German re-unification. Other countries were in need of German financial help and its ability to form winning coalitions within the European Council. For instance, Poland, which used to be particularly concerned about German power, has turned out to be an advocate of German leadership. In November 2011 Poland's Foreign Minister, Radek Sikorski, declared in Berlin that he feared German inaction more than German power.[8] (Five years earlier Minister Sikorski was still comparing the Russian–German Nord Stream gas pipeline project to the 1939 Molotov–Ribbentrop Pact envisaging the partition of Poland between Nazi Germany and the Soviet Union.)

Of course, German policies since the outbreak of the crisis have also been severely criticized for their 'pigheaded brinkmanship' and the 'economic colonization of Europe'. Angela Merkel has been portrayed as Adolf Hitler, and her country accused of building a Fourth Reich. The relentless bashing of Germany in some parts of the media could not but influence public opinion. In a 2013 Harris poll,

88 per cent of respondents in Spain, 82 per cent in Italy and 56 per cent in France said Germany's influence in the EU was too strong. However, even the most fanatical Germanophobes seemed to recognize that Germany was the only actor able to restore some degree of hierarchy and order in Europe and put the continent back on the path of reintegration (albeit a direction much detested by Euro-sceptics).

However, it is far from certain that Germany is indeed able to reintegrate Europe on its own. It is even less certain that Germany has any intention to take on this role. Why would it entertain hegemonic ambitions if its policy of economic integration and diplomatic multilateralism has elevated it to its highest ever status within Europe? It makes no sense for Germany to return to a path that brought it such misery in the past.

Of course, Germany may change its intentions and embrace the imperial project; it may also become an empire by default. In fact, sophisticated analysts such as Ulrich Beck already talk about an 'accidental' German empire.[9] However, Germany can only act as an engine of reintegration if it commits sizeable resources for realizing a plausible European project. So far Germany's policies towards Europe have shown little sense of direction and scant willingness to invest huge sums of money in any common endeavour. After the fall of Lehman Brothers, Germany declared that the virtual guarantee extended to other financial institutions should come from each country acting separately, not by Europe acting jointly. This has put weaker economies within the euro-zone under enormous strain and contributed to the outbreak of the euro crisis. Throughout the crisis Germany has done enough to prevent the collapse of the euro, but little to alleviate structural differences between stronger and weaker economies. For instance, it agreed to the creation of the European Stability Mechanism envisaging the injection of capital directly into banks, yet the proposed funds were insufficient and subject to rigid conditions. Put bluntly, German policies were aimed more at punishing than assisting. The Fiscal Compact Treaty, for example, imposes severe sanctions on countries that fail to reduce excessive debt by 5 per cent a year. It also obliges member states to share their budget plans with EU institutions. Critics such as George Soros argue that slashing budgets is bringing down demand, driving up unemployment, undermining consumer confidence and reducing growth. An alternative approach would be to abandon the rigid punitive approach and relieve crisis-stricken countries of the excessive interest-rate burdens that are hampering their growth.[10]

Reintegration

History shows that for an empire to be successful the metropolis needs to support its vast peripheries or else they will cheat and rebel. The imperial centre ought to offer something tangible and attractive for the peripheries to accept its authority and comply with its wishes. A functioning empire cannot just issue arbitrary laws and punish those who fail to obey. Successful empires need a plausible civilizational mission, which in this particular case would mean a vision of a prosperous Europe, and not just a prosperous Germany. So far, Germany has failed to spell out such a vision and to back it up by required resources. Germany pushed forward policies that may have worked for it a decade ago, but are producing disastrous economic, social and political consequences for debtor countries at present. Greek governments may have been 'cooking up' their statistics, but it was Germany (together with France) who designed the flawed euro system. It was also Germany (again with France) who first broke the euro-zone rules regarding budgetary discipline; the very rules it originally suggested. Germany has ultimately succeeded in putting its finances under control, and this should certainly be applauded. However, Greece shrank its structural deficit by 12 per cent between 2009 and 2011 – twice as much as Germany during a longer period under far better conditions.

In view of the above, one can have little sympathy for Germany's self-righteous rhetoric, which resembles sanctimonious Protestant preaching, with little space for economic and political reasoning. Greece may well be the greatest 'sinner', but Germany cannot just demand that the country slashes budgets for public schools and hospitals with no clear prospect of economic recovery. The same argument applies to Germany's policies towards other European countries currently in trouble.

To be successful as an empire, Germany would need to generate security and stability, whereas its current policies achieve the opposite, regardless of presumably good intentions. To be successful as an empire, Germany would also need to be more tolerant and generous. Creating the European Stabilization Mechanism with a relatively small and capped budget is not enough. Nor is it sufficient to create a symbolic fund aimed at combating youth unemployment in Southern Europe. To be seen as a benevolent rather than coercive power, Germany would need to endorse significant financial transfers to countries with failing economies, allow a moderate increase in inflation, reduce its trade surplus and act as a consumer of last resort in order to help indebted economies grow their way out of recession. In short, to be a successful empire, Germany needs to create a system of meaningful incentives for its European partners and reduce its reliance on austerity and sanctions.

German policy-makers are fond of saying: 'When outsiders ask us for leadership, what they mean is our money.' This shows that they do not really understand that leadership always involves sacrifices and not just privileges. German policy-makers are also fond of saying: 'We are being criticized for whatever we do.' This shows that they do not fully comprehend that with power comes responsibility. German power is indispensable to making Europe prosperous, but this power ought to be exercised in consultation with other Europeans, for the benefit of the entire continent. Otherwise Germany will not be able to orchestrate European reintegration. Throughout the crisis, Berlin has acted with its domestic rather than European public in mind, casting its own policies as virtuous and those of other states as flawed. Most Europeans do not want to hear German lessons in morality; they want to see Germany help to get Europe out of the crisis – a crisis for which Germany also bears some responsibility.

As we have seen, Germany has proven to be a reluctant and poorly skilled hegemon. This means that reintegration along an imperial pattern is not a credible prospect. With the EU weakened by the crisis, there is no other actor that could single-handedly reintegrate the continent.

Conclusions

Current visions of reintegration are likely to fail because they are dependent on nation states' support, and they do not evoke enthusiasm of citizens across Europe. European states are reluctant to delegate the powers of their cabinets, parliaments, courts and banks to the EU. Even if some of them are prepared to do so, they are unable to agree on a comprehensive institutional framework to please all and not just some of its current members. Germany could put its weight behind the reintegration of the continent, but it is clearly unwilling to bear the costs of such an endeavour. Citizens across the EU seem to have little interest in the overall European institutional architecture and are uneasy about a possible resurgence of the German empire, however benign and enlightened. They are obviously concerned about their jobs, security and pensions, and some of them have begun to think that the EU has placed these in jeopardy. Those who are more positive about the EU wonder whether it is worth investing sizeable resources in a project that has a good chance of failing in the end. To return to our automobile analogy, would anybody buy an expensive car that has a 20 per cent chance of engine failure? Probably not, yet that is a conservative estimate of the chances of the EU becoming dysfunctional and marginalized by key political and economic actors. In short, reintegration can hardly occur without addressing the deficit of confidence. This confidence is not likely to be regained by offering more of the same under the slogan 'there are no alternatives'. It is time to 'call the EU's bluff' and to show that there are plausible alternatives to the current mode of integration.

4

Vision

Advocates of European integration are fond of propagating a 'bicycle' maxim: Europe should never stop moving forward or else it will begin to topple. Ralf Dahrendorf, a leading European intellectual and politician, was not convinced by this maxim: 'I often cycle in Oxford,' he once remarked, 'and if I stop pedalling I do not fall; I simply put my feet on the ground.'

Dahrendorf's reasoning may help us in projecting Europe's future after the failure of ambitious integrative schemes. Europe will not necessarily come a cropper; it will probably adopt a more pragmatic, modest and gradual approach to integration. But even if apocalyptic scenarios are not likely to materialize, this does not mean that Europe will remain as it is. The weakening of the EU will doubtless accelerate changes already fostered by technology, social modernity and markets. Over the next decade or two we will witness a new pattern of relations among European actors; the political geography of Europe is also likely to change and so will the balance of political and economic forces. European institutions will be weaker and European networks will be stronger. Some European states will face competition from their powerful regions, while others will need to devolve considerable powers to large and more prosperous cities. Divergence between European states will also increase, with some resembling failed states while others will be more reminiscent of empires. States will also integrate unevenly: some will join only a few selected integrative frameworks, while others will try to be on board (if not at the helm of) many European clubs and networks. NGOs will become stronger and less territorially bounded. Citizens of Europe will have ever-more multiple loyalties and associations and less trust in traditional communal hierarchies and values. Europe will look like a complicated puzzle without a clear institutional structure, legal order and ideological consensus. Is any kind of integration possible in a Europe of plural political allegiances, overlapping jurisdictions and flourishing socio-cultural heterogeneity? My answer is yes, but we must modify our vision of integration by

Vision

embracing genuine pluralism and diversity. I will argue that a more flexible, decentralized and hybrid Europe offers enormous opportunities, and should not be seen as leading to Westphalian anarchy.

The ghost of Westphalia

It is often said that the EU has rescued Europe from the Westphalian condition. As Joschka Fischer put it in his famous speech at Humboldt University in 2000: 'The core concept of Europe after 1945 was and still is a rejection of the European balance of power principle and the hegemonic ambitions of individual states that had emerged following the Peace of Westphalia in 1648.'[1] The fall of the EU could therefore imply a return of devastating power politics and possibly also war. The crisis has clearly reinforced the Westphalian scenario, and so the President of the European Commission, José Manuel Barroso, has warned against exploiting the EU's weakness:

> Let me say this to all those who rejoice in Europe's difficulties and who want to roll back our integration and go back to isolation: the pre-integrated Europe of the divisions, the war, the trenches, is not what people desire and deserve. The European

75

continent has never in its history known such a long period of peace as since the creation of the European Community. It is our duty to preserve it and deepen it.[2]

Barroso, Fischer and many others use the words integration, Europe and the European Union (or its predecessor the European Community) synonymously. This is somewhat problematic. The Westphalian analogy is also problematic. States were never as equal and sovereign as the Peace of Westphalia had envisaged. Anarchy, hegemony and war are not exclusive features of that era either. No wonder some scholars talk about the 'Westphalian myth'.[3] That said, it is important to query whether the fall of the EU will not bring back the type of power politics associated with earlier periods. After all, recent outbursts of nationalism and partisan squabbles generated by the euro crisis recall the ghosts of Westphalia. In Europe today small states once again fear the domination of large states. Weaker states again conspire behind the back of stronger states and try to form coalitions in order to balance local hegemons. Germany is the most obvious suspect, but Portugal also feels pressure from its large neighbour Spain, Belgium lives in the shadow of France, Slovenia sees Italy as a local hegemon and Lithuania is uneasy about

Poland. Populism and xenophobia are also on the rise with no regional authority to keep them in check. All these developments are indeed disquieting and reminiscent of the most traumatic events in Europe's history. However, history is not likely to repeat itself, for several reasons.

For a start, the EU has not been the only actor assuring peace in Europe: NATO and the United States have also played important parts and so has the Organization for Security and Cooperation in Europe, for instance. Interstate conflicts in contemporary Europe are no longer about territory and borders, but about the shape of European institutions and the abuse of agreed laws. Although European states still have national armies, their purpose is not to wage wars with other EU member states (even though the British and the French, in particular, frequently deploy their forces in different parts of the world). The size of most European armies is shrinking rather than growing, which obviously constrains states' capability to engage in military adventures. The old-type politics of balancing and band-waggoning is virtually impossible in the highly interdependent environment of contemporary Europe, in which security, economic and social issues are fused and unbound.

In other words, the Westphalian brand of politics

is difficult to practise at present and it makes little sense. The modern states of Europe have come to realize that their power and well-being are affected more by the state of their economies and 'human capital' than by territorial acquisitions, aggressive international coalitions and various forms of military adventurism. Can bullying and conspiring really enhance the power of any post-industrial European state? Would Hungary attempt to re-gain territories populated by Hungarians after seeing what misery such a policy inflicted on Serbia? Can European states afford to take each other on when China, India, Turkey and Russia are waiting to take advantage of the continent's internal squabbles?

The euro crisis has undermined trust between states and generated fear and mutual suspicion. Cooperation is more difficult as a consequence, with weaker states more eager to cheat and stronger states more eager to punch above their weight. The pompous rhetoric of pride and glory is again on the rise, propagating national myths and manifesting parochial arrogance. However, this does not mean that we are back to Westphalia. Not all conflicts lead to war, not all national ambitions are about imposing regional domination, and not all inter-state coalitions are about dividing Europe into competing spheres of influence. The relationship

between European states has turned sour and chaotic over the last few years, but none of these states
are willing or able to practise old-style geopolitics
à la Metternich or Bismarck (let alone *à la* Hitler
or Stalin). Globalization has prompted a shift from
nation states to market states, to use Philip Bobbitt's
expression; market states have less interest in traditional military expeditions.[4] Europeanization has
also transformed states. As Christopher Bickerton
has persuasively argued, in contrast to classical
nation states, governments of EU member states
understand their power and identity as dependent
upon their belonging to a wider group or community.[5] This not only shapes their threat perceptions,
but also gives them a distinctive social purpose: the
need to search for cooperation and compromise in
Europe. Even American critics of Europe such as
Robert Kagan have observed that Europeans favour
peaceful responses to problems, preferring negotiations, diplomacy and persuasion to coercion. As
Kagan has cynically remarked, Europeans seem to
'live in a self-contained world of laws and rules and
transnational negotiation and cooperation'.[6]

I'm not suggesting that war is no longer con-
ceivable in Europe simply because of cascading
interdependence and the spread of post-materialist
values. What I am saying is that the fall of the EU

will not necessarily make Europeans more prone to violence and coercion. If the EU breaks up in a chaotic manner there might be an outburst of mutual recriminations, but this does not mean a return to 'la géopolitique de grand "papa"' (old-style geopolitics), to use François Heisbourg's expression.[7]

The Westphalian scenario assumes the existence of strong states fully in charge of their respective territories. Those who demand repatriation of powers from Brussels assume that this will make their states strong and sovereign again. They are likely to be disappointed. As Alan Milward's historical analysis has demonstrated, European integration has strengthened rather than weakened states in Europe.[8] The European Community has been an indispensable part of the nation state's post-war reconstruction. Without it, the nation state could not have offered its citizens the same measure of security and prosperity which it has provided, and which has justified its survival. With the fall of the EU the reverse is likely to happen. States will find it increasingly difficult to fend off global pressures, maintain social contracts and defend their policy failures. Other actors, both public and private, are likely to gain in importance and compete for institutional powers and political allegiances. Such a scenario suggests a step towards not a new Westphalian era, but a new medieval one. But what exactly does neo-medievalism mean for Europe?

The rise of plurality and hybridity

New medievalism symbolizes a break with the Westphalian era, and the failure of its modernist institutional embodiment: the EU. However, it does not suggest a 'back to the future' scenario with a computerized version of the Middle Ages. It only suggests that the future structure and exercise of political authority will resemble the medieval model more than the Westphalian one. The latter is about concentration of power, hierarchy, sovereignty and clear-cut identity. The former is about overlapping authorities, divided sovereignty, differentiated institutional arrangements and multiple identities. The latter is about fixed and relatively hard external border lines, while the former is about fuzzy borders with ample opportunity for entrance and exit. The latter is about centrally regulated redistribution within a closed national or European system. The former is about redistribution based on different types of solidarity between various transnational networks. The latter is about strict rules, commands and penalties, while the former is about bargaining, flexible arrangements and incentives.[9]

Nor does new medievalism mean the death of European nation states; rather it implies further transformation of these states and the increased importance of other polities, be they large cities or regions. NGOs will also grow in importance, some of them defending certain values such as environmental or minority rights, while others will represent corporate or consumer interests. The result will be a multiplication of various hybrid institutional arrangements, and increased plurality of political allegiances. This is a trend that has been noted by academics for some time. The expected fall of the EU will only accelerate it and make it more pronounced. In some fields, such as defence, states may well remain the principal actors, but in other fields, such as market regulation, social policy or internal security, numerous local or transnational actors, private or public or mixed, will have a chance to gain in importance. Even democracy is likely to be less territorial with the media and NGOs monitoring politicians across Europe's borders more skilfully than national parliaments.

The projected scenario may sound novel to students of the EU, but not to students of globalization and social change. For years the digital revolution has been generating major transformations in production, communication, competition and security. The post-modern revolution has generated alterations in our core values, notions of interest and social hierarchies. How many young men are still willing to die for their country? Do many people still believe that states can control financial markets? How many members of parliaments are able and willing to represent the interests of their voters? The EU crisis is a small episode in this on-going historical spectacle, but it is also quite symptomatic. After all, the EU was an important instrument in the hands of European nation states. With no EU to help or blame, they will find it difficult to justify their formal powers, for the legitimacy of these states rested on three pillars – their key provision of welfare, democracy and administration – all of which are now trembling, leaving other actors likely to step in.

For a few initial decades after World War II, European states could legitimate their extensive powers by claiming that they were the only providers of impressive welfare provisions made possible by continuous economic growth. However, these states have seen little growth in the last two decades and the welfare system is now bankrupt in some states and shrinking in others. Unemployment is rising (especially among young people), and so is poverty (especially among older people). It is hard to imagine any significant economic improvement in the coming years, meaning that citizens' trust in their states as economic agents is likely to be severely tested. With state pension systems in disarray in some countries, private pension funds are becoming increasingly important. In some countries specialized NGOs (civic and religious) have proven more effective in alleviating poverty than governments. The privatization of education and health systems is progressing alongside the marketization of these important services. Access to quality hospitals, schools and housing is now determined more by the rules and managerial skills of large cities or regions than states. New private chains have invested huge funds in public hospitals in Berlin and Hamburg. In Denmark regional governments have acquired extensive powers to organize health care delivery. And there are numerous further examples of states losing their grip over the welfare of their citizens.

States do not perform any better as democratic agents. Even though it is often argued that democracy, unlike the economy, can only be run by nation states with their crystallized *demoi* and workable systems of representation, the state-centred model of representative democracy, with its formal reliance upon parliaments, parties and elections, is increasingly unpopular and dysfunctional. Public trust in parliaments and parliamentarians is very low following a series of scandals that even affected Westminster, the 'mother' of parliamentary democracy. Political party membership is falling dramatically, while the average age of party members is rising. If it is true that the average member of the UK Conservative Party is about 68 years old,[10] one wonders whom this party represents. Electors can still choose their representatives freely, but these representatives are not free to reverse their countries' policies. Nor is there any evidence that the results of successive elections determine where the power, profits and privilege are located. Even in such a relatively well-functioning state as Sweden, the proportion of citizens who think that politicians have lost touch with those they govern has risen from 35 to 70 per cent over recent decades. Not surprisingly, therefore, non-state democratic representation is being developed in and around various interest and pressure groups, the work-place or the corporation, social movements, clubs and advocacy groups. Local communities are also becoming important democratic actors. Elections to the regional parliaments of Catalonia or Lombardy are now more crucial for many citizens than national parliamentary elections. Leading politicians run for mayoral posts in such large cities as Paris, London or Warsaw. Elections, parties and parliaments – the pillars of state-centred democracy – are also becoming less crucial to the functioning of democracy. As John Keane has persuasively argued, extra-parliamentary, power-scrutinizing mechanisms led by the media, think tanks or polling agencies are proliferating, constantly keeping elected politicians 'on their toes'. We live in an age of 'monitory democracy' and traditional forms of parliamentary representation are in retreat.[11] As a result, European states can no longer claim to be the only site offering meaningful forms of popular representation, accountability and participation.

States were also said to be the most crucial administrative agents, but one wonders whether this is still the case. In some (chiefly Northern European) states there has been a sweeping privatization, deregulation and marketization of national administrative systems. Agencies independent of the central government have proliferated to regulate and oversee various branches of administration. Public–private partnerships have blossomed. All these reforms have made the state just one of many administrative agencies. In other (chiefly Southern European) states similar public management reforms have been obstructed by informal corporatist and clientelistic networks. Administration has remained essentially in the hands of the state, but it continues to be politicized, oversized and unresponsive. With public debt mounting, the public administrations have become the prime victims of rather random budgetary cuts, and one wonders if they will ever recover from the shock.

States have also lost administrative powers through the process of territorial devolution and decentralization. The most pronounced examples here are Belgium, the UK, Italy and Spain, but traditionally centralized states such as France and Poland have also decentralized their administration. Belgium, which used to be a regionalized unitary state, has been transformed into a highly decentralized federal state comprising communities and regions. In the UK devolution has led to the creation of separate regional civil services that are involved in policy development. Institutional and fiscal decentralization have gone hand in hand. Local governments have been granted either greater taxing powers or more discretion in using assigned central resources. Moreover, decentralization has gone hand in hand with a new management style giving local governments more choice and flexibility and reducing hierarchical steering. These developments have encouraged innovative regional initiatives such as the Metropoli-30 network of leading industrialists and politicians in Spain's Basque Country, which led to the successful overhaul of the region's shipping, rail, urban-infrastructure and cultural strategies.

So far, the process of territorial devolution and decentralization has not led to the break-up of any state, but it has produced what John Loughlin has called 'hybrid states', in which central and local authorities share not only administrative but also political powers, over which they need to bargain.[12] The outcome of this bargaining process can no longer be taken for granted, meaning that some states may lose their primacy in European politics. This may be prompted either by secessionist tendencies of such powerful local units as Scotland, Catalonia and Lombardy or by a major governance failure of central administration. (A combination of both of these factors can also be envisaged.) Belgium went 588 days without a formal government after the 2010 political crisis, and the paralysis delayed the structural reforms expected of a country with one of the highest debts per capita in the EU. Italy has had emergency governments since 2011 that lack meaningful political consensus, and are unable to command their civil service. In the summer of 2013 a political storm ensued after it was revealed that the civil service had deported a Kazakh dissident's wife and six-year-old daughter without informing the Minister of the Interior.

Not all European states are faced with secessionist regions or are as dysfunctional as Italy or Belgium. The Swedish welfare system is much sounder than its Greek counterpart. Youth unemployment rates are alarming in Spain, but not in Austria or Germany. The democratic problems of Denmark are of a different scale and nature than those of Hungary. This means that some states are likely to fare better than others, which only reinforces the argument about the rising diversity, pluralism and hybridity across the continent. States unable to cope with a variety of internal and external shocks would have to share powers with other units, be they local or transnational. Not only the health of individual states will matter, but also their size. The majority of states in the EU are small, if not tiny, and they may face fierce competition from Europe's largest and most successful cities and regions.

Large urban agglomerations and 'global cities', to use Saskia Sassen's expression, are currently seen as the most likely candidates to fill the political and administrative vacuum resulting from the loss of power at the national level.[13] They have become the greatest beneficiaries of the de-territorialization process generated by globalization, digitalization, privatization and deregulation. Some experts are already talking of the metropolitan revolution in Europe. London, Paris, Milan and Frankfurt are not only the engines of the European economy and the key centrs for trade and investment, but they also progressively assume political, social and cultural functions traditionally performed by nation states. Moreover, they are the sites for global management functions and key generators of technological innovation. They are also key sites of television, radio and press, shaping political agendas and cultural trends. Modern cities operate transnationally through a variety of trans-border networks, often ignoring traditional interstate diplomacy. Their inhabitants are also transnational; large cities host both most jet-flying CEOs and ordinary migrants. Unlike regions, they do not compete with states for territory and cultural loyalty. They are actors from a different, super-modern universe, promoting new forms of management and administration, utilizing opportunities created by a digitized global economy and exploring alternative solutions to social and environmental challenges. Their problems and interests hardly coincide with those of nation states.

At times they join state-sponsored initiatives, especially those envisaging multiple stakeholders and the fusion of public and private ownership. At other times, they work with other cities outside the state-led framework in a mode resembling the medieval Hanseatic League. And yet at other times, they join forces with global markets or transnational NGOs to oppose certain laws or policies of their countries.

Not only subnational actors such as cities and regions, but also supranational ones such as global digitalized markets and free trade blocs will take advantage of the loss of power at the national level. Mixed entities are also emerging in the form of cross-border regions or of what Parag Khanna called parastatals: transnational wealth funds, extractive companies, utilities, administrative and judicial centres, export-processing zones and urban-development authorities.[14]

The developments I've described set out a Europe of numerous complex networks and circles. The relationship between territory, authority and rights is likely to be significantly changed, not by design but as a consequence of governance failure and transnational pressures. As always, winners and losers will emerge from this change, with as yet unclear power and location. Although the envisaged scenario is driven by social modernization and technological innovation, the system of rule it is likely to generate will be familiar to historians. Plural political allegiances, multiple and overlapping jurisdictions, a polycentric system of governance, cascading cultural and institutional heterogeneity were known in Europe throughout the Middle Ages. The new arrangement may well be more hip and mobile, but it will not be particularly unusual. Will integration be possible in such a neo-medieval Europe?

A new approach to integration

There is no commonly accepted definition of integration. Most students see it as the voluntary creation and maintenance of regional institutions by states in Europe. It envisages comprehensive legal treaties, ever-greater convergence across ever-more policy fields and central steering from Brussels. Europe emerging from the current crisis will only have a few of these ingredients. In this book I have sketched out a vision of weak central European institutions with states either unable or unwilling to give support to Brussels. Plurality, heterogeneity and hybridity will be the norm with no comprehensive legal framework structuring relations among a variety of actors across different policy fields. For

followers of Jean Monnet this neo-medieval scenario heralds the end of integration. However, there
are good reasons to question such a conclusion.

Paradoxically, reducing the size and power of
European institutions may prove to be a blessing
rather than a curse for integration. After all, the
EU found itself in trouble because its institutions
claimed ever-more powers without a popular mandate. States were not necessarily the best agents of
integration. They tried to use the EU for their own
parochial ends without committing any significant
resources to common endeavours. States also had
little trust in each other, and so they generated mon-
strous treaties and cumbersome decision-making
procedures to bind each other. Diversity and heterogeneity are normal states of affairs in complex
polities and there is no reason to insist on ever-
greater convergence across the vast European space.
Diversity is an engine of social development and
economic innovation. Diversity, i.e. pluralism, is a
pillar of democratic order. Integration recognizing
local conditions and rejecting rigid hierarchical
blueprints may prove more effective in coping with
problems of complex interdependence.

In short, it would be good to envisage a method
of integration suitable for the neo-medieval environment. One does not need to engage in abstract

theories of collective action to see that Europeans are unlikely to defend their labour rights, social provisions, health and food safety standards without advanced cooperation. Immigration, trade, transport, energy and environmental degradation are also easier to address through some form of integration. The problem is that the EU has proved not particularly effective in addressing many of these challenges and it has lost public support. It's time to consider a different way of integrating.

What would the proper integration archetype imply, and how will it differ from the current one? Below are four observations that could be called Mitrany principles. David Mitrany's work from the 1940s to the 1970s not only anticipated the current problems caused by 'states-led' integration, but also proposed original solutions for integrating complex, interdependent and transnational polities of the sort that we are witnessing today.[15]

First, successful integration would have to be carried out by multiple actors and not just by states. As long as states are self-appointed gatekeepers of integration, it is difficult for transnational networks to assume any independent role. However, the failure of the EU may well break the monopoly of states and allow cities, regions, professional associations and NGOs to join old, or form new, transnational integrative networks. States are likely to take part in these networks, to a lesser or greater degree, depending on the issue handled by a given network. For instance, one can hardly imagine a network dealing with Europe's immigration or security without the participation of states. However, non-state actors should be allowed to play a meaningful role in all networks in order to prevent states and their bureaucracies (including the military and intelligence sectors) from cultivating bad habits.

Second, the new approach would envisage integration along functional rather than territorial lines. Different networks could integrate in different policy fields such as trade, energy, human rights, immigration or security. The current emphasis on territory rather than tasks lumps together states regardless of their actual needs and situations. Moreover, it creates an artificial border of Europe with privileged insiders and outsiders who are discriminated against. In reality, different tasks concern a different territory and therefore require diversified spatial arrangements. For instance, some parts of Europe are more concerned with maritime traffic than others. The ability of individual actors to join a given integrative network also varies and should be better recognized by the new paradigm. For example, Ukraine may not be able to join a European network dealing with immigration, but it may join a network dealing with energy or the environment.

Third, the structure of integrative schemes should be polycentric and not hierarchical. It should resemble numerous horizontal rings rather than a single vertical pyramid. This is because task-oriented integrative networks would evolve without any overall institutional blueprint producing a neat architecture. Networks would have a different scope and shape depending on the challenge they were supposed to address. Networks would have to comply with European and national laws, but no single European centre would oversee them, let alone dictate specific policies. For instance, the Schengen system dealing with Europe's borders used to be independent of the EU, but the Amsterdam Treaty incorporated Schengen into the EU's overall structure. Schengen is now a core part of EU law and all EU member states with the exception of the UK and Ireland are legally obliged to join it. This proposal suggests reverting back to the original arrangement, provided the Schengen system survives.

Fourth, governance of integrative networks would have to be flexible, plurilateral and diversified. This is because different policy fields require different types of membership, different modes of engagement and different mixtures of incentives and sanctions.

Some fields, such as the Internet, are moving rapidly and they constantly require new innovative solutions. Other fields, such as human rights, require clear benchmarks and consistent policies. In the fields of industrial competition, taxation or customs sanctions are more appropriate than in the fields of immigration or the environment, where incentives in terms of training and material equipment are more suitable. Governance in the present-day EU is largely about constructing and maintaining the European centre of authority. The new vision of integration should emphasize problem-solving capacities, and this requires rules that are able to cope with a complex and ever-changing environment.

A musical metaphor may help us to grasp the difference between the current and the proposed paradigms of integration.[16] The current paradigm, which we can call EUphony, resembles what in music is called monophony: a musical texture made up of a single unaccompanied melodic line. The proposed paradigm resembles polyphony: a style of musical composition employing several simultaneous but relatively independent melodic lines. Polyphony relies on so-called 'counterpoints' which envisage the relationship between voices that are harmonically interdependent, but independent in rhythm and contour. Numerous musical lines that sound very different and move independently from one another sound harmonious when played simultaneously. Polyphony envisages interaction, respect, differentiation and improvisation. A sub-category of polyphony, called homophony, exists in its purest form when all the voices or parts move together in the same rhythm, as in a texture of block chords. However, more loose and simple variants of polyphony are frequent.

Polyphony was initially banned by the Church because of its alleged secular, unruly and thus 'devil-ish' features, but it became increasingly popular during the European Renaissance and formed the essence of Baroque music. The contemporary guard-ians of EUphony also castigate flexibility, plurality and differentiation as devilish. States are determined to preserve their monopoly over integration and insist on playing monophonic music. The problem is that their performance over the past few years has generated chaos, or, if you wish, cacophony, and it's time to think about a change of tune.

Conclusions

Europe turned neo-medieval by default, not by design. It was not supposed to be that way. EU officials and most of Europe's politicians have been promoting an 'ever-closer union' and transferring ever-more powers to Brussels. But when we look around we see cascading cultural as well as economic heterogeneity and citizens' resistance to rule by Brussels. The same officials and politicians who got us into the current mess insist that there is no alternative to their vision of European integration. But their vision did not pass the reality test, and it is utterly unsuitable for the Europe of today. It is time to put our feet on the ground, as Dahrendorf argued, and embrace a new vision of integration.

There is no need to stigmatize neo-medievalism. Neo-medievalism is driven by economic interdependence and technological innovation and not by the demons of nationalism. The threat of a Westphalian scenario of war and anarchy has not been found credible. Neo-medievalism does not preclude effective governance, but effective governance in a complex and differentiated environment will be less about automatic implementation of commands from the centre and more about bargaining and networking among European, national and local actors, public and private. The key concepts of such governance are self- and co-regulation, public and private partnership, cooperative management and joint entrepreneurial ventures. Nor does neo-medievalism preclude a sound system of the rule of law; however, there will be no one single law maker and court system for the whole of Europe. Clubs or networks responsible for the provision of a specific class of public goods will set up their own jurisdictions to oversee their affairs.[17]

Of course, this does not necessarily mean that Europeans will cooperate, let alone integrate. To do so they will need to be won over by a more plausible model of integration than the one envisaged by Berlin or Brussels. The alternative I'm proposing involves flexible integration along functional lines as opposed to the dogged pursuit of a European super-state. The networks that would emerge from this neo-medieval style of integration will not be fully fledged polities; they will be organizations designed to address particular needs and perform specific tasks. It is precisely these kinds of honed and diverse networks that Europe so badly needs.

5

Practising Polyphony

For most students of European politics the EU is a symbol of integration; to them its demise implies disintegration. However, it is difficult to deny some basic facts: the EU performs poorly at present and it has lost the support of most of Europe's citizens. The EU also seems unable to reform itself. In effect, it became a hindrance to, rather than a facilitator of, integration. In other words, the EU may well be doomed, but this is not all bad news for European integration.

Citizens who have lost trust in the EU are not necessarily happy with the performance of their nation states. Only very few of them ask for the raising of fences vis-à-vis other Europeans. For most, cooperation, rather than conflict, is the preferred option. They also know that a divided Europe is easy prey for non-European powers and global speculators.

That said, a dysfunctional EU is not worth investing in. Integration ought to be given another chance, this time with no EU at the helm.

The problem is that the EU has become too big to fail. Policy-makers may not be happy with its performance, but they are scared of jumping into the unknown. Therefore they keep it on life support, but since the prospect of success is small, they treat the rescue as a low-cost operation. Such a policy of muddling through may delay the EU's imminent demise, but it will not address its structural deficiencies, while creating a false feeling of security and stability. Benign neglect will turn into blind neglect. Moreover, the policy of muddling through is by its nature conservative and hostile to any innovation. The policy rests on the assumption that things are not as bad as critics argue, and serious reforms are likely to prove counter-productive if not dangerous.

Technically speaking, it may be possible to make the EU work. Banks that were 'too big to fail' are now being compartmentalized and divided into smaller, more accountable units. A possible failure of one unit no longers pose a threat to the entire banking system. The EU could undergo a similar operation. There are currently more than thirty European agencies and bodies spread across the entire continent and dealing with such diverse issues as vocational training, food safety, border controls or judicial cooperation. Most of them have regulatory tasks, but they also provide technical expertise and networking between national and European authorities. They receive some funds from the EU, but they are independent bodies with their own legal personality. Resources and prerogatives of these functional agencies could be significantly beefed up, while those of the EU's central institutions could be downgraded. The European Commission could be transformed into a kind of mega-regulatory agency responsible for the single market. The European Council could concentrate on setting some basic standards of access, transparency and accountability for these various regulatory bodies. The European Parliament, possibly under a different name, could do what it does best, a kind of auditing and monitoring of regulatory agencies with no pretensions to act as a sovereign pan-European representative assembly.

The role of EU agencies has indeed been upgraded over recent years, but the change proposed here is much more dramatic and, for a variety of political and legal reasons, it is highly unlikely that it will ever be undertaken. The European Commission may be down, but it is not yet out; it will insist on acting as a quasi-government for Europe. Powerful member states will continue to use the EU as a vehicle for their own national policies. Most of the weak member states will keep the EU because it gives them a seat at the decision-making table, however symbolic. The body of EU law would be difficult to amend or repel. In short, the EU will formally stay as it is, but it will gradually lose its usefulness and vitality. It will become an institutional decoy to rubber-stamp decisions taken outside of it. Unless there are some powerful external shocks forcing dramatic changes, a spectacle of false pretentions can continue for a long time. EU leaders will call for another 'reflection period', they will subsequently start a new round of inter-governmental negotiations that will last for many years and in the end only propose some minor cosmetic changes to the existing institutional arrangements. Citizens will not be invited to cast their vote for or against any dramatic options. UK Prime Minister David Cameron has promised an 'in or out' referendum by the end of 2017, but it is not clear what 'out'" would imply exactly.[1] Nor is it certain that the Conservatives will still be in power in 2017 and that any successor government will keep Cameron's promise. If Syriza wins the next Greek parliamentary elections there might also be a referendum in Greece on the issue of membership of the euro-zone. However, one or two exits from the current structures will not break the EU as such.

This does not mean that the EU will recover and become an effective means for coping with Europe's economic and political problems. Dormant institutions do not solve real problems; they only provide a cover for inaction or for actions that are not seen as legitimate. However, behind-the-scenes manipulation will be disclosed sooner or later by disillusioned whistleblowers. Occasional market failures, migratory pressures, energy shortages or pandemics will continue to batter the continent and will require collective European responses. Political and economic entrepreneurs will form spontaneous alliances and networks to address their specific concerns, be they in the field of transportation, trade, the environment, competition, health or social policy. They are most likely to ignore or bypass dormant EU institutions. Some functional European agencies mentioned earlier may gain in importance and seek further autonomy from the EU. They will begin to operate as clubs and networks, as Giandomenico Majone calls them.[2] These bodies will proliferate in response to new policy challenges in individual functional fields. Some European laws will be formally suspended or repelled, while others will be ignored by transnational networks creating their own independent jurisdictions. Initiatives to liberalize key economic sectors such as services or to amend rules regarding transport or industrial competition will be coming from clubs and networks rather than from the European Commission. The Commission will be allowed to administer various functional arrangements such as external trade, but it will not be allowed to act as a meta-governor. The European Council will become just one among several other decision-making bodies in Europe. Large cities and regions will have their own meetings and administration to coordinate common endeavours. The European Parliament will be paralysed by internal divisions between pro- and anti-EU parties, and between MEPs representing creditor and debtor states. In short, the EU may not be formally dissolved, but it will become less powerful, relevant and coherent. In time, it will become toothless and useless.

Such a development does not herald the end of European integration; in fact it heralds a revival of integration, albeit in a different form and scope. Diversity will be embraced, and hierarchy will be reduced. More emphasis will be placed on voluntary functional associations and less on territorial governance. States will no longer be the primary drivers of integration, but rather these will be

European cities, regions and NGOs supported or even pressed by firms and citizens. Europe's governance structure will look not like a pyramid, but like a 'junction box' with numerous points of interaction and intersection.[3]

I called this new mode of integration polyphonic, in contrast to the current EUphony or even cacophony. A polyphonic Europe will embrace the basic principles of democracy – plurality and self-government. It will also embrace the basic principles of effective governance: functional coordination, territorial differentiation and flexibility. The current EUphony obstructs most of that.

Defenders of the current status quo are likely to insist that only a quasi-federal Europe is able to punch above its weight in global affairs. This is nonsense. Europe was the most effective international actor in the field of external trade because member states voluntarily decided to pool their resources in this particular functional field. By using their common trade leverage they were able to achieve many political and security objectives. The EU Common Foreign and Security Policy (CFSP), by contrast, has achieved very little because member states were not prepared to pool their resources in this field. They repeatedly voted against each other in the United Nations, and they carried out most of their security operations outside of the EU framework, through informal coalitions of the willing, contact groups or bilateral initiatives. The creation of the office of the High Representative for Foreign Affairs and Security Policy or of the External Action Service has changed little in this respect. If the CFSP was useful at all, it was in providing a networking platform for discussing European foreign affairs. But this has never led to a proper European army or a European ministry of foreign affairs.

A polyphonic Europe with no strong centre but a variety of functional integrative networks will not be able to 'bribe' and punish reluctant actors, conduct secret negotiations and manipulate international institutions. This will presumably remain the domain of nation states. However, such a Europe would be well suited to creating institutional structures and setting up rules of legitimate behaviour. It could act as a model power showing other actors that European norms can also work for them and providing incentives for adopting these norms.

Defenders of the current status quo will also argue that a complex system composed of numerous clubs and networks will not be transparent and accountable.[4] They will point to the likely problems of pan-European supervision and coordination. They will be concerned about legitimizing complex polities and institutional arrangements. They will worry that European clubs and networks will not allow free, let alone equal, access of citizens.

These concerns are justified, but with some important qualifications. First, networks are not 'floating islands' (*îles flottantes*) operating above the law and free from any coordination and supervision. Networks will be subject to the laws of the countries in which they operate and also to their own statutes. And as noted earlier, numerous European laws and regulations are also likely to persist. These laws and regulations would have to guarantee certain standards of openness, fairness and transparency. Second, self-regulation is often a more effective ordering principle than the central rule by decree. Likewise, central commands are not necessarily the most effective in providing coordination and steering; shared aspirations and positive cooperative experiences represent a better foundation of harmony. Third, the size and functional scope of a unit matter; namely a huge pan-European unit such as the EU with prerogatives spanning across different functional fields requires a different kind of oversight and legitimacy than a relatively small functional unit responsible for transport or food safety only. For instance, a failure of a food safety agency to enforce its standards may lead to the dismissal of its board without causing a pan-European constitutional crisis. Fourth, power in a neo-medieval Europe will be de-concentrated, dispersed, divided or fragmented. There will be much less need for special arrangements to put brakes on the centre because there will be no clearly identified, hierarchical centre to balance and check. Fifth, there are various ways of securing account-ability. Complex networks tend to escape formal parliamentary scrutiny, but they are subject to a variety of informal controls that are less present in hierarchical systems. Networks usually watch each other and publicize abuses of power. Networks are also subject to the usual scrutiny by the media and NGOs. Sixth, it is easier to reform individual functional networks than a large multi-purpose institution such as the EU. How many times has the Common Agricultural Policy (CAP) been criticized, but left unreformed because European decision-makers linked the reform of the CAP to other complex institutional issues on the EU agenda?

This is not to deny the challenges ahead, but to point out the basic fact that large territorial systems run from a single centre also have their problems. As we have seen in the case of the EU, the centre is often detached from local concerns and it lacks basic sources of legitimacy. One-size-fit-all policies are not particularly suitable for a complex and diversified European environment. The ability of central hierarchical systems to secure coordination and discipline is often illusory. Of course, it will be important to prevent the emergence of various 'authority holes' leaving certain firms and citizens without jurisdiction and protection. However, the absence of central steering may open the door to more effective, flexible ways of governance recognizing local conditions. Decision-making competencies can be shared by actors at different levels rather than monopolized by European (or member states') executives. Governance in its essence is about the maintenance of collective order and the pursuance of collective goals, but there are various ways of achieving these. Besides, Europe is already a highly complex polity, and a 'jump' towards medieval polyphony would be less dramatic than it may appear. In any case, there is no need to apply stricter standards of efficiency, transparency and accountability to the neo-medieval Europe than to the EU Europe.

The major problem with clubs and networks pertains not to efficiency, transparency and accountability, but to their possible disconnection from civil society. Networks tend to operate in a technocratic manner, but their actions often have political, if not moral, implications. Who will decide which values ought to be given priority and which policies ought to be adopted? And how? So far, there are no plausible answers to these questions. One possible solution has been offered by Amitai Etzioni: integrative networks would have to engage in moral dialogues which go beyond negotiations of facts or interests and concern mutual perception of the common good.[5] These dialogues can be messy and without clear outcomes, warns Etzioni, but they can stimulate a sense of community without which integration can only be superficial, if not decorative.

It goes without saying that notions of the common European good cannot be egocentric, let alone xenophobic. For integration to succeed, the definition of the common good would have to acknowledge the otherness within and outside Europe. This is the basic premise of cosmopolitanism propagated by Zygmunt Bauman or Ulrich Beck. Tolerant interaction among Europeans is the prerequisite of any integration, and Europeans should also be open to interact with if not embrace other civilizations in the world. Further, if we follow Etzioni's dictum, institutional integration should go hand in hand with moral integration.

These are all ambitious prerequisites, but there is no need to think in absolute terms. Moral integration is about a normative discourse that recognizes plurality and otherness. It is not about drafting a European equivalent of the Ten Commandments. There is no guarantee that Europeans will simply follow the rational logic of integration in certain fields, but equally there is no need to assume irrationality on their part. Public support for individual networks may vary, but legitimacy is a relative concept, and the benchmark set up by the EU is very low indeed. Abandoning the ambition of an ever-closer union with ever-stronger European institutions and embracing instead genuine diversity, plurality and decentralization may well require a 'Copernican' revolution in our thinking about integration. However, upholding the status quo is not a viable option. Polyphony may be a medieval invention but it is well suited to the neo-medieval realities of today.

Besides, it is important to have realistic expectations of what integration can actually accomplish. Democracy and capitalism have their own problems, and European integration can only influence them in a marginal way, hopefully for the better. Nor can we hope that integration will get rid of international conflicts; at best it can create conditions under which peace and security are more likely. This does not undermine the importance of integration in cases where it enhances our capacity to cope with mounting challenges. The EU has repeatedly generated expectations that it has been unable to meet. This is one of the reasons for its decline, but, as I have argued here, integration will carry on and it will serve Europe well.

Further Reading

The crisis of the EU has generated a plethora of articles, but few books so far. Some of the most in-depth and timely analyses have appeared on the websites of European think tanks such as the European Council on Foreign Relations or Bruegel. National institutes and foundations such as the Greek ELIAMEP or the German Friedrich-Ebert-Stiftung have also issued valuable analyses. *Foreign Affairs*, *Current History*, *Journal of Democracy* and other popular academic journals have published special clusters devoted to the crisis. Fortunately there is no shortage of books in English analysing Europe's history and the history of European integration.

Those interested in Europe's *longue durée* should read Norman Davies' monumental *Europe: A History* (Oxford: Oxford University Press,

1996) or the more recent *Europe: The Struggle for Supremacy, 1453 to the Present* by Brendan Simms (London: Penguin, 2013). A collection of essays edited by Anthony Pagden, *The Idea of Europe: From Antiquity to the European Union* (Washington, DC: Woodrow Wilson Center Press; Cambridge: Cambridge University Press, 2002), examines multiple European identities from ancient Greece to the end of the twentieth century. My favourite books on Europe's modern history are Perry Anderson, *The New Old World* (London: Verso, 2011), Tony Judt, *Post-War: A History of Europe since 1945* (New York: Penguin, 2005) and Mark Mazower, *Dark Continent: Europe's Twentieth Century* (New York: Allen Lane, 1998).

Those interested in learning more about the history of European integration are recommended to read Alan Milward's *The European Rescue of the Nation State* (London: Routledge, 1992), Andrew Moravcsik's *The Choice for Europe: Social Purpose and State Power from Messina to Maastricht* (Ithaca, NY: Cornell University Press, 1998) and Luuk van Middelaar's *The Passage to Europe: How a Continent Became a Union*, translated by Liz Waters (New Haven, CT: Yale University Press, 2013). A fascinating account of the origin and development of the EMU is offered by Harold

James' *Making the European Monetary Union* (Cambridge, MA: Harvard University Press, 2012).

Over the past two decades, books on the EU's functioning have mushroomed, but they are of very uneven quality. The best comprehensive treatment of the topic is offered by two edited collections: Erik Jones and Anand Menon's *The Oxford Handbook of the European Union* (Oxford: Oxford University Press, 2012) and Helen S. Wallace, Mark A. Pollack and Alasdair R. Young's *Policy-Making in the European Union*, 6th edition (Oxford: Oxford University Press, 2010). International aspects of European integration are covered superbly in a volume edited by Christopher Hill and Michael Smith: *International Relations and the European Union* (Oxford: Oxford University Press, 2011). David P. Calleo in his brilliant *Rethinking Europe's Future* (Princeton, NJ: Princeton University Press, 2001) locates the European project in the context of global economic competition. Joseph H.H. Weiler's *The Constitution of Europe* (Cambridge: Cambridge University Press, 1999) is a special treat, especially for readers with a legal background.

At the beginning of the twenty-first century the EU's appeal is still powerful, as exemplified by Mark Leonard's *Why Europe Will Run the 21st Century* (London: HarperCollins, 2005) and Jeremy Rifkin's

The European Dream: How Europe's Vision of the Future Is Quietly Eclipsing the American Dream (New York: Tarcher/Penguin, 2004). However, with the passage of time more sombre analyses have started to warn against a possible backlash. The most insightful are Paul Graham Taylor's *The End of European Integration: Anti-Europeanism Examined* (London: Routledge, 2008), Neil Fligstein's *Euro-Crash: The EU, European Identity and the Future of Europe* (Oxford: Oxford University Press, 2008) and Giandomenico Majone's *Europe as the Would-be World Power: The EU at Fifty* (Cambridge: Cambridge University Press, 2009).

Some of the best analyses of the origins and implications of the current crisis have been published by Polity Press: Ulrich Beck's *German Europe* (2013), Anthony Giddens' *Turbulent and Mighty Continent: What Future for Europe?* (2013), Jürgen Habermas's *The Crisis of the European Union: A Response* (2012) and Simon Hix's *What's Wrong with the European Union and How to Fix It* (2008). Also worth consulting is Ivan Berend's *Europe in Crisis: Bolt from the Blue?* (London: Routledge, 2012) and an interesting collection of essays, *The Greek Crisis and European Modernity* (Basingstoke: Palgrave Macmillan, 2013), edited by Anna Triandafyllidou, Ruby Gropas and Hara Kouki.

Notes

Prologue

1 Christopher Hill, 'The Capability–Expectations Gap, or Conceptualizing Europe's International Role', *Journal of Common Market Studies*, Vol. 31, No. 3 (1993), pp. 305–28.

Chapter 1 Crisis

1 Federico Rampini, 'La spirale delle tre crisi', *La Repubblica*, 7 October 2008; available at: http://www.repubblica.it/2008/10/sezioni/economia/crisi-mutui-8/rampini-7ott/rampini-7ott.html (accessed 5 December 2013).
2 Some of these were rectified between 2010 and 2013. The current account deficit has been reduced, the public sector has shrunk, and in terms of structural budget deficit (the Fiscal Compact criterion of fiscal discipline) Greece proved to be among the best performers in the euro-zone. However, social impli-

cations of these forceful economic adjustments have been devastating. See, for example, Loukas Tsoukalis, 'Markets, Institutions and Legitimacy', *Journal of Democracy*, Vol. 23, No. 4 (2012), pp. 47–53.

3 According to Eurostat data for 2012, the average working week in Greece is 40.9 hours, compared to 36.6 hours in France, 35.5 hours in Germany and 34.6 hours in Denmark. The statutory minimum paid annual leave in Greece is well below the EU and eurozone averages. Moreover, the OECD statistics show that during the years preceding the crisis (2000–7), GDP per employed person in Greece grew at 2.8 per cent annually, compared to 1.1 per cent in Germany.

4 The Panhellenic Socialist Movement (Pasok), which dominated the Greek political scene for more than three decades, received just 12 per cent in the 2012 national elections, and a year later support for it plummeted to around 6 per cent in the polls. The Coalition of the Radical Left (Syriza) became the second largest party in the 2012 elections with 27 per cent of votes. The winner, the New Democracy party, polled only 3 per cent more than Syriza (the former was created in 1974 and the latter only in 2004). It should also be noted that the extreme-right party, Golden Dawn, received nearly 7 per cent of the votes and the 2013 polls registered a further rise in public support for this party.

5 Portugal represented an intermediate case with its gross public debt amounting to 63.6 per cent of GDP. Greece may well have had an exceptionally high public sector debt, but its private sector debt

was much lower than those of Ireland and Spain. That is one of the reasons why Spain and Ireland ended up in a financial mess, when part of their huge private sector debt was transformed into public debt, after their governments stepped in to rescue their banking systems. See, for example, Heikki Patomäki, *The Great Eurozone Disaster: From Crisis to Global New Deal*, translated by James O'Connor (London: Zed Books, 2013) or Costas Lapavitsas, *Crisis in the Eurozone* (London: Verso, 2012).

6 The EU budget was around €140 billion in 2011, which was very small compared to the sum of national budgets of all then twenty-seven (now, with Croatia, twenty-eight) member states, which amounted to more than €6,300 billion. In other words, total government expenditure by the twenty-seven member states was almost fifty times bigger than the EU budget.

7 Simon Tisdall, 'Will the Eurozone Crisis Bring Europe Together – or Tear It Apart?', *Guardian*, 14 September 2011; available at: http://www.guardian. co.uk/commentisfree/2011/sep/14/european-union-jose-manuel-barroso (accessed 6 December 2013).

8 The Stability and Growth Pact (SGP) aims to facilitate and maintain the stability of the Economic and Monetary Union through fiscal monitoring of members by the European Commission and the Council of Ministers, and the issuing of a yearly recommendation for policy actions to ensure a full compliance with the SGP also in the medium term. The Six Pack covers not only fiscal surveillance, but also macro-economic

surveillance under the new Macroeconomic Imbalance Procedure. For details see: http://ec.europa.eu/economy_finance/economic_governance/index_en.htm (accessed 13 December 2013).

9 Barbara W. Tuchman, *The March of Folly: From Troy to Vietnam* (New York: Ballantine Books, 1985), p. 4.

Chapter 2 Disintegration

Portions of this chapter are drawn from my article 'Elusive Solidarity', which appeared in the October 2012 issue of the *Journal of Democracy*.

1 Interview for RBB-Inforadio on 13 September 2011. See also http://www.sueddeutsche.de/politik/merkel-o-merkel-warnt-vor-kontrollverlust-der-politik-1.1142713 (accessed 9 December 2013).

2 Cited by Tomasz Bielecki, 'Wojna Idzie?', *Gazeta Wyborcza*, 15 September 2011; available at: http://wyborcza.pl/1,75968,10290674,Wojna_idzie.html (accessed 9 December 2013).

3 Ivan Krastev, 'A Fraying Union', *Journal of Democracy*, Vol. 23, No. 4 (2012), p. 23.

4 *Future Scenarios for the Eurozone. 15 Perspectives on the Euro Crisis* (Berlin: Friedrich-Ebert-Stiftung, 2013), pp. 6–7; available at: http://library.fes.de/pdf-files/id/ipa/09723.pdf (accessed 9 December 2013).

5 I owe this analogy to Mark Leonard, with whom I was engaged in a fascinating project on Reinventing Europe run by the European Council on Foreign Relations. For details see: http://www.ecfr.eu/reinvention/home (accessed 9 December 2013). See also Mark

Leonard and Jan Zielonka, *Europe of Incentives: A Survival Strategy for the EU* (London: European Council on Foreign Relations, 2012), pp. 23–31.

6 Sebastian Dullien, *Why the Euro Crisis Threatens the European Single Market* (London: European Council on Foreign Relations, 2012), pp. 1–5; available at: http://ecfr.eu/page/-/ECFR64_EU_CRISIS_MEMO_AW.pdf (accessed 9 December 2013).

Chapter 3 Reintegration

1 'Six Ideas to Save the EU', *El País*, *Guardian*, *Gazeta Wyborcza*, *La Stampa*, *Süddeutsche Zeitung*, *Le Monde*, 24 April 2013; available at: http://www.theguardian.com/world/2013/apr/24/europa-six-ideas-save-eu (accessed 9 December 2013).

2 Hans-Werner Sinn, 'Why Berlin is Balking on a Bailout', *New York Times*, 12 June 2012; available at: http://www.nytimes.com/2012/06/13/opinion/germany-cant-fix-the-euro-crisis.html (accessed 9 December 2013).

3 Speech by President Barroso during the debate on the economic crises and the euro, European Parliament plenary session, Strasbourg, 14 September 2011; available at: http://europa.eu/rapid/pressReleases Action.do?reference=SPEECH/11/572&format=H TML&aged=0&language=EN&guiLanguage=en (accessed 9 December 2013).

4 Speech by Federal Chancellor Angela Merkel at the opening ceremony of the 61st academic year of the College of Europe on 2 November 2010; available at:

http://www.bruessel.diplo.de/contentblob/2959854/
Daten/ (accessed 9 December 2013).

5 PM David Cameron, EU Speech at Bloomberg,
23 January 2013: available at: https://www.gov.uk/
government/speeches/eu-speech-at-bloomberg (accessed 9 December 2013).

6 José Ignacio Torreblanca and Sebastian Dullien,
'What is Political Union?' (London: European Council
on Foreign Relations, 2012); available at: http://ecfr.
eu/page/-/ECFR70_POLITICAL_UNION_BRIEF_
AW.pdf (accessed 10 December 2013).

7 The term *Bundesrepublik Europa* has recently
been used by several commentators such as Stefan
Collignon, Niall Ferguson and Timothy Garton Ash.

8 Radek Sikorski, 'Poland and the Future of the European
Union', speech at the German Society for Foreign
Affairs, Berlin, 28 November 2011; available at:
http://www.mfa.gov.pl/resource/33ce6061-ec12-4da
1-a145-01e2995c6302:JCR (accessed 10 December
2013).

9 Ulrich Beck, 'Germany Has Created an Accidental
Empire', *Social Europe Journal*, 25 March 2013; avail-
able at: http://www.social-europe.eu/2013/03/germ
any-has-created-an-accidental-empire/ (accessed 10
December 2012). See also Ulrich Beck, *German
Europe* (Cambridge: Polity Press, 2013) and William
Paterson, "The Reluctant Hegemon? Germany Moves
Centre Stage in the EU', *JCMS Annual Review of the
European Union*, Vol. 49, Issue S (2011), pp. 57–75.

10 George Soros, 'The Tragedy of the European Union
and How to Resolve It', *New York Review of*

Books, 27 September 2012; available at: http://www.
nybooks.com/articles/archives/2012/sep/27/tragedy-
european-union-and-how-resolve-it/ (accessed 10
December 2013).

Chapter 4 Vision

1 Joschka Fischer's speech at Humboldt University
in Berlin, 12 May 2000; available at: http://www.
cvce.eu/obj/speech_by_joschka_fischer_on_the_ulti
mate_objective_of_european_integration_berlin_12_
may_2000-en-4cd02fa7-d9d0-4cd2-91c9-2746a
3297773.html (accessed 10 December 2013).
2 José Manuel Durão Barroso, the State of the Union
address 2013, European Commission – SPEECH/
13/684 11/09/2013; available at: http://europa.eu/
rapid/press-release_SPEECH-13-684_en.htm (accessed 10 December 2013).
3 See Andres Osiander, 'Sovereignty, International
Relations and the Westphalian Myth', *International
Organization*, Vol. 55, No. 2 (2001), pp. 251–87;
or Stéphane Beaulac, 'The Westphalian Model in
Defining International Law: Challenging the Myth',
Australian Journal of Legal History, Vol. 8 (2004),
pp. 181–4.
4 Philip C. Bobbitt, *The Shield of Achilles: War, Peace
and the Course of History* (New York: Knopf, 2002),
pp. xxvi–xxvii, also pp. 811–20.
5 Christopher J. Bickerton, *European Integration:
From Nation-States to Member States* (Oxford:
Oxford University Press, 2012), pp. 12 and 14.

6 Robert Kagan, *Paradise and Power: America and Europe in the New World Order* (London: Atlantic Books, 2004), pp. 3 and 5.

7 François Heisbourg, 'Sécurité: l'Europe livrée à elle-même', *Politique Étrangère*, Vol. 59, No. 1 (1994), pp. 247–60.

8 Alan Milward, *The European Rescue of the Nation State* (London: Routledge, 1992), pp. 2–3.

9 I spelled out the contrast between these two models in my book *Europe as Empire: The Nature of the Enlarged European Union* (Oxford: Oxford University Press, 2006), pp. 7–20.

10 There is some debate over this figure. See Brian Wheeler and Chris Davies, '"Swivel-Eyed Loons" or Voice of the People?', BBC News, 21 May 2013; available at: http://www.bbc.co.uk/news/uk-politics-22607108; Ross Clark, 'End of the Party – How British Political Leaders Ran Out of Followers', *Spectator*, 14 September 2013; available at: http://www.spectator.co.uk/features/9019201/the-end-of-the-party/; Andrew Rawnsley, 'The Numbers That Add Up to Trouble for All Political Parties', *Observer*, 13 July 2013; available at: http://www.theguardian.com/commentisfree/2013/jul/13/political-party-membership-coalition-labour; Tim Bale and Paul Webb, 'Members Only: View of the Conservative Party's Rank and File', The Political Studies Association; available at: http://www.psa.ac.uk/insight-plus/members-only-views-conservative-party%E2%80%99s-rank-and-file. (All sources accessed 13 December 2013.)

11 John Keane, 'Monitory Democracy?', in *The Future of Representative Democracy*, edited by Sonia Alonso, John Keane and Wolfgang Merkel (Cambridge: Cambridge University Press, 2011), pp. 212–13.

12 John Loughlin, 'The "Hybrid" State: Reconfiguring Territorial Governance in Western Europe', *Perspectives on European Politics and Society*, Special Issue: Reconstituting Political Order in Europe, West and East, Vol. 10, No. 1 (2009), pp. 51–68.

13 Saskia Sassen, *Territory, Authority, Rights: From Medieval to Global Assemblages* (Princeton: Princeton University Press, 2006), pp. 54–69.

14 Parag Khanna, 'The Rise of Hybrid Governance', *New America Foundation*, 19 October 2012 (pages not enumerated). See also Parag Khanna, *How to Run the World: Charting the Course to the Next Renaissance* (New York: Random House, 2011).

15 David Mitrany, *A Working Peace System* (Chicago: Quadrangle Books, 1966; first published in 1943), pp. 5–10.

16 The term *polyphony* has been used in European studies. See for instance, Janie Pélabay, Kalypso Nicolaïdis, and Justine Lacroix, 'Conclusion. Echoes and Polyphony: In Praise of Europe's Narrative Diversity', in *European Stories: Intellectual Debates on Europe in National Contexts*, edited by Justine Lacroix and Kalypso Nicolaïdis (Oxford: Oxford University Press, 2010), pp. 334–362.

17 Alessandra Casella and Jonathan S. Feinstein, 'Public Goods in Trade: On the Formation of Markets and Jurisdictions', *International Economic Review*, Vol.

43, No. 2 (2002), pp. 437–56. Also Alessandra Casella and Bruno Frey, 'Federalism and Clubs: Towards an Economic Theory of Overlapping Jurisdictions', *European Economic Review*, Vol. 36 (1992), pp. 639–46.

Chapter 5 Practising Polyphony

1 Hugo Dixon, *The IN/OUT Question: Why Britain Should Stay in the EU and Fight to Make It Better* (forthcoming), chapter 1.

2 Giandomenico Majone, 'Rethinking European Integration after the Debt Crisis', UCL, The European Institute, Working Paper 3/2012, pp. 22–5.

3 The term 'junction box' was coined by Helen Wallace in her chapter 'The Institutional Setting', in *Policy-Making in the European Union*, edited by Helen Wallace and William Wallace (Oxford: Oxford University Press, 2000), p. 36.

4 As Neil Walker has observed, accountability is a particularly serious problem in a 'crowded institutional context, where popular affinity is contested or diluted and lines of responsibility are blurred'. See 'Flexibility within a Metaconstitutional Frame', in *Constitutional Change in the EU: From Uniformity to Flexibility?*, edited by Gráinne De Búrca and Joanne Scott (Oxford: Hart, 2000), p. 11.

5 Amitai Etzoni, *Political Unification Revisited: On Building Supranational Communities* (Boston: Lexington Books, 2001), p. xxxii.